CAN BUSINESS SAVE THE EARTH?

Innovating Our Way to Sustainability

Michael Lenox and Aaron Chatterji

STANFORD BUSINESS BOOKS

An Imprint of Stanford University Press • Stanford, California

Stanford University Press
Stanford, California

© 2018 by the Board of Trustees of the Leland Stanford Junior University.
All rights reserved.

No part of this book may be reproduced or transmitted in any form or by any
means, electronic or mechanical, including photocopying and recording,
or in any information storage or retrieval system without the prior written
permission of Stanford University Press.

Special discounts for bulk quantities of Stanford Business Books are available
to corporations, professional associations, and other organizations. For details
and discount information, contact the special sales department of Stanford
University Press. Tel: (650) 725-0820, Fax: (650) 725-3457

Printed in the United States of America on acid-free, archival-quality paper

Library of Congress Cataloging-in-Publication Data

Names: Lenox, Michael, author. | Chatterji, Aaron, 1978- author.
Title: Can business save the Earth? : innovating our way to sustainability /
    Michael Lenox and Aaron Chatterji.
Description: Stanford, California : Stanford Business Books, an imprint of
    Stanford University Press, 2018. | Includes bibliographical references and
    index.
Identifiers: LCCN 2017041096 (print) | LCCN 2017045491 (ebook) |
    ISBN 9781503606197 (e-book) | ISBN 9780804790994 (cloth : alk. paper) |
    ISBN 9781503606197 (ebook)
Subjects: LCSH: Business enterprises—Environmental aspects. | Technological
    innovations—Environmental aspects. | Industrial management—
    Environmental aspects. | Sustainable development.
Classification: LCC HD30.255 (ebook) | LCC HD30.255 .L46 2018 (print) |
    DDC 338.9/27—dc23
LC record available at https://lccn.loc.gov/2017041096

Cover design: Christian Fuenfhausen
Typeset by Motto Publishing Services in 11.75/16 New Baskerville

In memory of my father, James Lenox,
who cultivated my passion for the environment

In honor of my father, Manas Chatterji,
who encouraged me to keep
reading, writing, and thinking

CONTENTS

PREFACE AND ACKNOWLEDGMENTS

Climate change and our broader sustainability challenge pose a critical threat to our ability to flourish on this planet. Addressing this challenge will require substantial innovation across a wide number of industrial sectors that promise to disrupt existing technologies and business models. Such an audacious project will require active leadership by business as well as the deep involvement of others—scientists, inventors, investors, customers, policy makers, activists, among others—who impact the ability of our system of innovation to thrive. This book is about how we can catalyze innovation through the actions of this broad set of stakeholders to address our sustainability challenge.

Through our research and teaching at the University of Virginia (UVA) and Duke, respectively, we find reasons to be both concerned and optimistic. Concerned because so much of what we observe in the realm of business and sustainability today seems woefully insufficient to meet the challenge before us. Optimistic because we observe an enterprising spirit in our students and alumni every day. We have seen firsthand the impact that passionate innovators and entrepreneurs can have in inventing a new future, especially one that promises a more sustainable planet that will allow humans to flourish. Because of our experience, we choose optimism over defeat.

As scholars, we have long been interested in the interface between business and the broader public sphere. Trained as economists, we have benefited from our time on the faculty of leading business schools. We have come to appreciate the complexity of businesses and the importance of what is referred to in the academic literature as non-market strategy— the ways business addresses the diverse set of institutions and stakeholders that impact their organizations outside the normal market context.

We have also benefited from being passionate scholars and observers of innovation and entrepreneurship. This intermingling of business strategy, public policy, and innovation has provided us a different perspective on our sustainability challenge than that of many who see the issue as simply a question of getting large corporations to internalize the negative externalities of pollution and other environmental impacts. Appreciating our innovation imperative opens a broader lens to examine climate change and sustainability and suggests a plethora of policy options, both public and private, beyond the current stalemate around whether to regulate greenhouse gas emissions.

In pursuing this project, we have benefited greatly from conversations and engagements with our academic colleagues, business leaders, policy makers, and leaders of nongovernmental organizations. We wish to recognize our various co-authors and collaborators who have shaped our thinking on sustainability over the years: John Ehrenfeld, Andrew King at Dartmouth, Chuck Eesley at Stanford, Michael Toffel at Harvard, David Levine at Berkeley, Kira Fabrizio at Boston University, Gary Dushnitsky at London Business School, Scott Rockart at Duke, and Jeff York at Colorado. We also wish to recognize the support and influence of the community of scholars that make up the Alliance for Research in Corporate Sustainability.

In addition, Lenox benefited from conversations with colleagues at Stanford University during a visiting professorship as well as feedback received at academic seminars at Michigan, Cornell, University of North Carolina, INSEAD, University of Southern California, Colorado, Brigham Young University, Miami, and Nanyang Technological University in Singapore. Chatterji benefited from engagements during his time at the Harvard Business School and the White House Council of Economic Advisers.

We wish to recognize the support of our colleagues and students at the Darden School of Business at UVA and the Fuqua School of Business at Duke. They have greatly influenced our thinking and provided inspiration for our efforts. Both schools provided financial support for this project for which we are most grateful. The Batten Institute at UVA, in particular, provided significant support in terms of both time and talent, including the convening of an innovators' roundtable of leading corporate sustainability leaders. A special thanks goes to Erika Herz from the Batten Institute, who has been a passionate scholar and advocate for our book and the broader sustainability challenges that we discuss within.

This book would not have been possible without the expert research assistance provided by Becky Duff and Nusrat Jahan. Thank you for your numerous contributions. They have greatly enhanced the end product. Thanks as well go to Margo Beth Fleming, Olivia Bartz, and the entire team at Stanford University Press. In addition, we thank reviewers David Vogel at Berkeley and Glen Dowell at Cornell. We greatly appreciate all of your suggestions and feedback. The book is much improved due to your feedback and guidance.

Last, but certainly not least, we wish to thank our families: Macy Lenox, Ben Lenox, and Haley Lenox and Neely Shah,

Anya Chatterji, Deven Chatterji, and Kieran Chatterji. The writing of this book has been a multiple-year affair. Your patience and understanding are greatly appreciated. Your love and support kept us moving forward to complete the project.

Michael Lenox
Charlottesville, VA

Aaron Chatterji
Durham, NC

CAN BUSINESS SAVE THE EARTH?

Chapter 1

BUSINESS AS SAVIOR

THE EARTH IS IN TROUBLE. The existential threat posed by a changing climate and environmental "unsustainability" is leading to dire predictions about the future of its land, its sea, and its people. The threat will likely unfold slowly, but once it gains momentum, it might be impossible to stop. The impact could be enormous, as significant as any war or plague; in fact, wars and plagues may be direct outcomes of climate change and environmental degradation.

So who will save the Earth? The usual suspects are missing in action. Government policy makers, particularly in the United States, cannot even agree on how serious the threat is and are hindered by seemingly intractable political differences. The US government has expressed its intent to exit the Paris Climate Agreement. International bodies lack the requisite authority to compel nations to act in the interests of the collective good. As individuals, our attempts at conservation, however well intentioned, will simply not be enough.

This ominous scenario has left many people looking for a savior armed with a silver bullet: a group of individuals and organizations with the scale, power, and resources, and ultimately the will, required to save the Earth. Enter the business community. We hear about the transformative power of business every day. The private sector, leveraging the power of markets and incentives, has created jobs, improved health, reduced poverty, and improved our general welfare. Perhaps our best hope for the Earth now rests on charismatic chief executive officers (CEOs), ingenious innovators, and miracle-working entrepreneurs who will deliver a sustainable future. We need to align the drive to create, to invent anew, with our generational challenge to save the Earth. Because, as the thinking goes, where there is a will (and a buck to be made), business will find a way.

Let's stop and take a breath. The magic of markets and the promise of innovation are offered up as solutions to every contemporary social issue, from education to health care to the environment. Can it really be that simple? Can an unleashed private sector solve a problem that has vexed policy makers for years? Can the innovative spirit that underrides our most dynamic markets drive innovation in sustainable technologies? Can business be the savior of our imperiled planet?

For many observers, the whole idea is preposterous. The private sector, with its voracious appetite for resources and development, is *responsible* for much of the predicament we face, so this line of thinking goes. The problems facing the natural environment stem directly from business interests running roughshod over the public good. The Earth's only savior will be an emboldened public sector, which will protect our planet from the negative effects of private-sector greed.

Who is right? Quite simply, neither. It is highly unlikely that business can or will save the Earth on its own. But governments cannot do it on their own either. Love them or hate them, business and markets are catalysts for innovation and change. Our environmental challenge is the wickedest kind of problem imaginable: complex, interconnected, and requiring massive collective action. A systematic challenge needs a systemic solution, the kind that is the hardest to build and sustain. We will need leading women and men, from all sectors and all corners of the Earth, to play a starring role.

This book is about unlocking the innovative potential of markets and the roles we all need to play, whether we run large companies, power the fountainhead of invention, finance impactful investments, or simply spend our hard-earned money at the grocery store every week. We will find important supporting roles for universities, all levels of governments, and nongovernmental organizations (NGOs). Together, a team like this, diverse and unwieldy as it might seem, could drive systemic change and actually save the Earth. The stakes could not be higher.

Business as Savior?

Many environmentalists have traditionally viewed the business community, particularly big business, as the primary source of—not the solution to—the critical environmental challenges that we face. There are some important facts on their side. Industrial pollution persists in the face of pressures on businesses to reduce costs and improve margins. Electric utilities pump out millions of tons of carbon dioxide each year, contributing to a rise in greenhouse gas concentrations in the atmosphere and increasing the potential for global climate change. Toxins accumulate in our bodies from chemicals embedded in the products we use. And our societal obsession with consumption is fueled by a half-trillion-dollar advertising industry geared at getting us to consume ever more.[1]

But there are also important reasons why business will have to be part of the solution if we are ever to make progress on our environmental challenges. Individual companies are some of the largest and most influential institutions in the world. If we compare the gross domestic product (GDP) of the largest countries to the revenues of the largest companies, forty-two of the world's one hundred largest economic entities are corporations.[2] Walmart, with $421 billion in revenue in 2010, ranks twenty-fifth, higher than the economies of Norway, Iran, and Austria. Shell, ExxonMobil, BP, and Toyota are among the largest fifty economies.[3] Overall, the forty-two companies in the Top 100 list generated the equivalent of 11% of global GDP.[4] The economic power of the leading global companies is too powerful to ignore. Businesses are arguably best positioned to generate and commercialize new sustainable technologies.

But will they take action? There are certainly opportunities for businesses to make a difference, whether greening their supply chains or providing the innovations that can accelerate a transformation to more sustainable technologies. But we have studied businesses long enough to know that they are complex organizations. They face multiple, sometimes conflicting, incentives. They operate in environments of high uncertainty and risk. Even the notion of a "sustainable" business or technology is hard to define. Sometimes the best of intentions causes more harm than good.

Consider the following example of a company that is a pioneer in its industry. A leading innovator. The first to break with orthodoxy and observe that global climate change is a real concern that needs to be addressed—a company that reenvisioned itself as "green." This company put its money where its mouth was—pledging to reduce its carbon emissions by 10% from 1990 levels in ten years, arguably a 50% reduction, given the firm's projected growth. It instituted an innovative internal cap-and-trade program to reduce those emissions, achieving these targets three years ahead of schedule and saving $650 million in the process. And the organization was an early investor and leader in clean technology, helping drive this new segment forward.

The CEO was widely hailed as a visionary and a leader in creating the socially responsible business of the future. He received a knighthood from Queen Elizabeth II. He received at least one prominent business school's highest honor for his work. His company also received numerous accolades. Fortune named it the number-one most admired company in its sector. The Dow Jones Sustainability Index called the firm number one among its peers. The Accountability Rating placed the company number one in the world across sectors. The Community's Corporate Responsibility Index ranked the firm number two in the world. The organization won the Dignity International Award for contributions to human dignity, won the Clarion Award for transparency in stakeholder relations, and was named a best place to work by *Working Mother* and *Essence* magazines.

The CEO: John Browne. The company: BP.

Missing from the description of accolades, of course, is that BP's Deepwater Horizon accident was one of the most damaging spills in history. Or that it operates in a sector, oil and gas, that is a major contributor to global warming. BP illustrates the perils of pinning our hopes on any single company or CEO. BP did indeed take a principled stance on climate change and made significant investments in alternative energy. It was in the vanguard on cap and trade of greenhouse gases and had significantly reduced its own emissions.

Despite its efforts to be a responsible steward, a string of accidents around North America has made BP a sustainability pariah.

Jim Rogers, formerly of Duke Energy, was another business leader trying to bring about a more sustainable future. He stood out from many CEOs, particularly in the energy sector, by supporting legislative efforts during the Obama administration to enact a comprehensive policy response to our sustainability challenges. Here was a business leader willing to accept, even requesting, regulations that might hinder his business in the short term because he believed that in the long term his company and the Earth would be better off. Ultimately, the pernicious politics of climate change killed the bill, and the world's largest economy remains stuck in an untenable status quo. But Rogers's example also demonstrates the potential for business leaders to become advocates for the kinds of public- and private-sector actions we will need to rise to this challenge. Business does indeed contribute to many of our sustainability challenges. But business also has tremendous potential to address them. Figuring out how to best harness the innovative power of companies is our task in the pages ahead.

Our Sustainability Challenge

To understand what business can and cannot do, it helps to understand the nature of the problem better. First, what do we mean "save the Earth"? Technically, Earth does not need saving. Our planet will be fine, thank you very much. It existed long before humans came about and will persist if humans disappeared from the planet. Not that it is likely that humans will go extinct. Fortunately, humans have proven to be an incredibly resilient species, able to adjust to and thrive in extreme environments across the globe. The real question is what will life on Earth be like for us if we fail to address the environmental challenges we face?

As John Ehrenfeld eloquently advocates in his book *Sustainability by Design*, our sustainability challenge is really a question of how we build a future where humankind can flourish. The common definition of "sustainable development" adopted by the Brundtland Commission is "development that meets the needs of the present without compromising the ability of future generations to meet their own needs."[5] In other words, a sustainable system is one that can perpetuate itself into the future. However, the sustainability of the system tells us little about the quality of life of those immersed in the system. How does one define the "needs" of today, let alone the needs of tomorrow? Is simply meeting those needs a sufficient goal for humanity?

To Ehrenfeld, sustainability, recast as "flourishing," suggests a system where individuals can achieve their full potential, living lives of fullness and meaning. Flourishing necessitates resilient natural systems that support not only our basic needs—food, water, shelter—but also provide sufficient resources and services to allow us to thrive, to achieve the potential of the human spirit. Ehrenfeld offers a beautiful vision for the future and one that accumulating evidence suggests is increasingly difficult to achieve. Many observers have expressed concern that our exponentially growing population is placing demands on natural resources and ecosystems that we cannot sustain and will likely hinder the flourishing of humankind. From the dawn of humans until the advent of the twentieth century, worldwide population grew to approximately 1.5 billion people. In the last century, that number doubled fourfold with six billion people welcoming in the new millennium. In the decade-plus since, we have seen well over another billion people added to the world and population growth continues unabated.

The need to feed this growing population places stress on existing farmland and requires the conversion of more and more land to agriculture, in some cases through deforestation or the irrigation of otherwise inhospitable land. The growing population creates greater stress on resources such as fresh water and increases demand for energy and other goods and services. The status quo is probably not sustainable. Natural systems rarely, if ever, can cope with exponential growth. Estimates for Earth's maximum carrying capacity vary widely, depending largely on how available resources are spread across the planet. With the current world population at 7.3 billion people,[6] some scientists believe that we have already exceeded the Earth's carrying capacity.[7]

The stresses such growth have placed on the natural environment are manifest all around us. Scientists are in near-universal agreement that we are experiencing atmospheric concentrations of carbon dioxide and greenhouse gases that have never been observed in human experience.[8] Most scientists agree that these concentrations are the result of anthropocentric activity, primarily the burning of fossil fuels to provide electricity and heat.[9] Evidence accumulates that, left unaddressed, greenhouse gases will continue to collect, creating the conditions for global climate change. We will see increasing average global temperatures, melting glacial and polar ice resulting in rising sea levels, and increases in the likelihood of extreme weather events like droughts, hurricanes, and flooding.[10]

A useful shorthand for what it might mean to "save the Earth" is helpful here. The Intergovernmental Panel on Climate Change (IPCC) has calculated a carbon budget under which we must limit our emissions to avoid the most dire consequences of climate change. If we exceed this budget, we will not be able to avoid a rise in global temperature of two degrees Celsius above the level that existed before the Industrial Revolution.[11] While two degrees may not sound like much, the impacts on global climate can be significant. While the economic impact of climate change is difficult to assess primarily due to the vast number of scenarios and variables, one team of researchers has developed a model that suggests a potential reduction of average global income of 23% by the year 2100.[12] The IPCC devotes an entire section in its *Climate Change 2014: Synthesis Report* to explain the limits of economic assessment, providing an "incomplete" potential loss range of 0.2% to 2.0% of global income if the approximately 2.5 degrees Celsius warming, compared to preindustrial levels, occurs.[13] Although they disagree on the absolute impact, they all seem to agree that with increased warming comes significant negative economic impacts and a decline in general welfare.

While global climate change attracts the most attention, and rightfully so, there are other stresses that are becoming increasingly evident. Fresh water is becoming ever more scarce in many parts of the world. By 2025, according to the United Nations, 1.8 billion people will live in countries or regions unable to provide access to water sufficient to support those populations, and two-thirds of the world could live under water stress conditions.[14] Up until 2017, the state of California experienced a prolonged period of drought that, in combination with a growing population, increased development, and the demands of agriculture, is creating a slowly unfolding crisis. Drastic restrictions are being proposed, and a political fight is boiling between the water needs of farms and the water needs of urban communities. The US military is increasingly worried that water shortages in hot spots in the world such as the Middle East will increase the likelihood of civil strife and war, which tend to only exacerbate resource scarcity.

In general, the US military views environmental crises as a critical part of its scenario planning for the future. For this reason the military has been one of the strongest voices about the risks of climate change in the United States. In an influential report published in 2015, the US military identified climate change as an immediate threat to "human security" and "the ability for governments to meet the basic needs of their populations." The report also lays out the most serious risks to each Combatant Command and estimates for the resources needed to respond to such threats.[15] These dire warnings remind us that our current trajectory threatens sustainability from several different directions, including through economics and through conflict over scarce resources.

The problems continue to multiply. For example, the nitrogen cycle is not well understood or appreciated by the general public. Many scientists believe that we are on the cusp of a significant environmental crisis. Nitrogen is ubiquitous in the environment and is maintained in balance by a number of natural processes. Nitrogen in fertilizers for farming finds its way into streams, rivers, and ultimately oceans, throwing off this delicate balance. Since preindustrial times, the amount of fixed nitrogen in the environment has doubled because of human activity.[16] The result is acidification and the destruction of ecosystems contributing to, among a number of problems, the loss of biodiversity.

The evidence suggests this is already occurring. According to the International Union for Conservation of Nature (IUCN), the current species extinction rate is estimated to be between one thousand and ten thousand times higher than what would occur naturally, with the total number of threatened species reaching 16,298.[17] Coral reefs are particularly threatened. The World Resources Institute (WRI) estimates that 75% of coral reefs around the world are currently under stress by local and global human activities. Rising ocean temperatures and bleaching due to climate change have contributed greatly to the demise of coral reefs. These vibrant ecosystems support thousands of diverse species of aquatic life such as lionfish, clownfish, and trumpetfish and several varieties of sharks, rays, starfish, and sea urchins. If nothing is done to protect the reefs, 90% of these ecosystems could be threatened by 2030. According to WRI, coral reefs protect more than ninety-three thousand miles of shoreline with ninety-four countries' economies benefiting from the tourism that coral reefs attract.[18] Similarly, stresses are at work on other valuable ecosystems such as rain forests, grasslands, and the tundra.

Finally, localized pollution remains a persistent challenge in many parts of the world. Urban smog, acid rain, and river pollution remain facts of life for many of Earth's residents. Beijing regularly experiences heavy smog resulting in an air-quality score that is two to three times higher than the level of particulate matter in the air deemed safe by the World Health Organization on any given day. Face masks have become ubiquitous on the streets of many cities in China.

Even in Western countries that have long regulated local pollutants, problems persist. In the United States, the Clean Air Act has helped to greatly reduce air pollution. Yet more than half of Americans, or 166 million people, live in areas that experience air-pollution levels that make the air dangerous to breathe.[19] Pollution from nitrogen and phosphorus runoff is causing algae blooms and dead zones in waterways across the country. The Environmental Protection Agency (EPA) estimates that one hundred thousand miles of rivers and streams; 2.5 million acres of lakes, reservoirs, and ponds;

and eight hundred square miles of bays and estuaries face water-quality issues because of nitrogen and phosphorus pollution.[20] Some 48% of Ohio's watersheds have been affected by nutrient pollution,[21] and pollution in the Chesapeake Bay has earned it a spot on the EPA's "dirty water" list. The biggest source of pollution in the bay watershed comes from agriculture, but the fastest-growing source is polluted runoff, which comes from urban and suburban areas.[22]

Our complex sustainability challenge is a result of interrelated factors and hard to address. It is often difficult to know where to start. But this much is clear. We need a huge change, not simply an incremental step, to save the Earth. The course we are on cannot be corrected without a major pivot. And even more daunting, this massive transformation must occur across multiple sectors at approximately the same time. These changes will upend entire industries, ranging from manufacturing to agriculture to transportation to energy. We are not simply one innovative battery away from achieving sustainability.

The Innovation Imperative

There are no easy fixes. Many scientists, policy makers, and business leaders argue that to address our sustainability challenges requires innovation on a massive scale. Simple calls to "cease and desist"—to stop engaging in activities that have negative environmental consequences—are neither realistic economically nor likely sufficient to drive us toward sustainability. Similarly, calls to simply reduce consumption, while sensible, are like the proverbial little Dutch boy holding back the floods by putting his finger in the dike. People will continue to demand products and services, and producers will provide them. Any reduction in per-person consumption needs to more than compensate for the increasing number of people in the world to reduce net impact. Absent wholesale changes in worldwide attitudes and consumption patterns, we need entirely new products, services, business models, and production processes that simultaneously create value to humans while minimizing, or even ameliorating, environmental impacts.

To illustrate this point, consider global climate change. An influential study by the Princeton Environmental Institute estimates that in order to keep carbon emissions *flat* over the next fifty years, we will need to trim our projected carbon output by roughly eight billion tons per year by 2060. The study's authors identify fifteen strategies to achieve these reductions, from wind, solar, and nuclear energy to energy efficiency and carbon capture. Importantly, they observe that no one strategy is sufficient. The upshot is that we must simultaneously innovate across multiple technologies and adopt multiple approaches if we have any hope of meeting this goal.

Some argue that we already have the technology necessary to address our sustainable challenges. Renewable energy is gaining momentum and, as a result, is starting to compete with fossil fuels. According to the REN21 *Global Status Report*, renewable sources provided 19% of global energy output in 2014.[23] Organic farming techniques demonstrate the viability of agriculture that does not overly rely on irrigation and fertilizers. Tesla and the introduction of electric vehicles by the likes of BMW and Nissan demonstrate that alternatives to gasoline-powered automobiles are viable. The technology exists, the argument goes; what we lack is the will to adopt.

We disagree. Technology cannot be considered in isolation from the broader socioeconomic system in which it is embedded. Innovation is not just invention—defined as the creation of something new. Innovation is the marriage of in-

vention and commercialization. For an innovation to be viable, it must create value for individuals who are ultimately
willing to subsidize the development, installation, and scaling
of a new technology. Solar cells and wind turbines are wonderful technologies. Innovation has helped improve their efficiency and lower the cost of their manufacturing—as much
as 200% in the case of solar cells from 2010 to 2015. This in
turn has attracted investment and helped spread adoption.
But it has not reached its potential or fully captured the
hearts and minds of the public.

What future can we predict for renewable energy if significant innovation in the use of fossil fuels keeps pace with renewable technologies? Consider July 11, 2008. The price of
oil hit $147 per barrel. As many worried about the impact of
high oil prices on economic growth; others quietly celebrated
the creation of an opportunity. Now was the time for renewables—solar, wind, biomass—to significantly shift our energy
portfolio. Investment in green technology surged. Numerous renewable energy start-ups emerged, and, in the United
States alone, investments in greentech start-ups reached a
high of more than $7 billion in 2008.[24]

Fast-forward five years. The price of oil dropped to $50
per barrel. Innovation in the energy sector has flourished—
just not in the way that technology optimists had predicted.
Advances in hydraulic fracking and horizontal drilling had
lowered the costs of extracting oil and gas from regions previously left fallow. In the United States, an energy renaissance
was under way. It was looking like the country would achieve
energy independence by 2017. By January 2015, the price of
gasoline in the United States was under $2 per gallon. The
price of natural gas had plummeted to $3 per million Btus
(British thermal units). Despite gains in solar technology,
energy produced by natural gas power plants continued to

be more cost effective. Projections released in the 2015 US Energy Information Administration (EIA) Annual Energy Outlook show the cost of electricity produced at a conventional combined-cycle natural gas plant ($/MWh [megawatt-hour])—put into service by 2020—will be on average 35% lower than that produced at a utility-scale solar photovoltaic (PV) installation (65% without tax credits).[25] Venture capital investment has consistently dropped since 2008, down to $2 billion in the United States by 2014.[26]

What went wrong (or right, depending on your perspective)? We argue that the success of an innovation is ultimately judged by the value it creates for some end user. Investment and adoption in renewable energy depend on a myriad of factors, including advancements in competing, mainstay technologies, specifically natural gas and oil. That brings us back to markets. Love them or hate them, markets are the way that most innovations express their value. As every entrepreneur knows, a new product or service is judged by the willingness of others to pay for her goods at a price that exceeds the entrepreneur's cost to produce them. Thinking about it this way casts innovation in a different light. The innovation imperative is to drive up the efficiency and drive down the cost of renewable energy to compete with fossil fuels. This goal can be achieved by improving the underlying technology—such as PV cells—or by innovating around any number of complementary technologies such as energy storage solutions (batteries), electrical distribution (smart grid technology), or business models (financing for residential adopters of solar panels).

The same innovation imperative exists for numerous other "sustainable" technologies: energy-efficient computing and electronics, low- or no-emission vehicles, green buildings and supplies. We define sustainable technologies as those products, services, business models, and production processes that reduce the environmental impact of these goods relative to other existing technologies. A sustainable technology in and of itself does not guarantee sustainability; rather, it promises to reduce the unsustainability of existing technologies.[27] By continuously innovating new sustainable technologies, however, we can reduce unsustainable practices such as natural resource depletion and environmental degradation and increase the prospects for future generations to flourish.

The Panacea Hypothesis

The innovation imperative is not without its critics. The prospect for innovators to save the day has led to what has been referred to as the "panacea hypothesis"—the belief that innovation is a cure-all to our sustainability challenge.[28] This has given rise to a cottage industry in hype about the emerging green economy—that "green is gold" and that sustainability will be the new growth opportunity for business. All we need to do is unleash our innovation capacity on our sustainability challenge, and all will be right with the world.

If only it were so simple. History is littered with the unintended consequences of new technologies promising to better the world. The automobile was heralded as an environmental good during its introduction at the turn of the twentieth century. In many ways, it was—at least when compared to the dominant form of transport at the time—horse-drawn carriages. The collection and disposal of manure was a serious environmental and public health concern, especially in major cities such as New York. Just how serious was the manure problem? In 1898, there were two hundred thousand horses transporting people around New York City, amounting to nearly five million pounds of manure a day.[29]

Consider a more recent example. In the 1980s, hydrofluorocarbons (HFCs) were heralded as replacements for chlorofluorocarbons (CFCs) and the solution to an observed decrease in stratospheric ozone concentrations over Earth's poles. CFCs (more commonly known by the DuPont brand "Freon") were widely used as a coolant in refrigeration systems and as a cleaning agent in a number of industrial applications. Once evidence accumulated that CFCs were a primary contributor to a growing hole in the ozone layer above Antarctica, forty-six countries signed an international treaty, the Montreal Protocol, pledging to phase out the hazardous technology. HFCs, as a substitute, were supposed to accelerate the phaseout of CFCs and lead to a reversal of the ozone hole. Problem solved, except HFCs had other undesirable properties. In particular, they are a potent greenhouse gas, increasing the likelihood of global climate change. HFCs are now scheduled to be phased out in the United States by 2030.

These historic examples teach us that we need to influence both the rate and direction of innovative activity. Simply *more* innovation is insufficient. We need different kinds of innovation. Furthermore, we need innovation that minimizes the risk of unintended consequences. To what extent can we expect businesses to provide both the extent and type of innovation necessary? Why would a business invest time and effort in a green product rather than, say, a new software game for smartphones or a new drug for male-pattern baldness?

The Business Response to Date

In recent years, we have seen evidence that business has turned a corner and is stepping up to the sustainability challenge. We have seen a proliferation of corporate sustainability initiatives. Companies have adopted inspiring value statements with respect to innovation and the environment that seek to not only reduce the company's environmental foot-print but also provide a healthier planet for employees, inves-tors, and the wider community. Microsoft, for example, states,

> Microsoft is committed to leveraging technology to solve
> some of the world's most urgent environmental issues, and
> focusing on key areas where we believe we can have the most
> positive impact. . . . We work to reduce our impact within our
> own operations, collaborate with our partners to take advan-
> tage of digital transformations that reduce their footprint,
> and support innovation, R&D, and policies that help create a
> more sustainable future.[30]

As another example, UPS states in its Committed to More program, "Our sustainability efforts are focused on doing more to protect the environment, more to enhance the econ-omy, more to develop empowered people, and more to con-nect communities worldwide."[31]

The position of chief sustainability officer reporting di-rectly to senior leadership has been created at leading compa-nies such as General Electric, DuPont, Nike, Google, AT&T, Walmart, and Coca-Cola. Numerous companies have adopted environmental codes of conduct, such as Responsible Care in the chemical industry, and are marketing and selling cer-tified, environmentally friendly goods and services through programs such as the Leadership in Energy and Environmen-tal and Design (LEED) Standard in the building industry and the US Food and Drug Administration (FDA) Organic Food Standard in the food industry.

Perhaps most important, businesses are measuring and reporting the environmental impact from their activities. In the last five years, we have seen a significant growth in the number of companies that publish annual sustainability re-ports detailing their emissions and impacts. In 2012, just un-

der 20% of the S&P 500 Index companies published sustainability reports. By 2015, it had increased to 81%.[32] According
to a 2014 report released by the World Wildlife Fund in partnership with Ceres, 43% of Fortune 500 companies set targets for greenhouse gas reduction, renewable energy, energy
efficiency, or a combination of these goals—60% of the Fortune 100 have set such targets.[33] This is critical because, as
the old business adage says, "what gets measured get managed." Companies are becoming increasingly sophisticated in
measuring their environmental footprint. Major consultan-
cies and accounting firms all have sustainability practices to
help managers on this front.

It is important that we recognize this as progress. Up until
the early 1990s, to the extent that businesses thought about
environmental issues at all, it was usually as a legal or regulatory issue to be addressed by corporate legal counsel. Compliance offices, typically referred to as Environment, Health,
and Safety (EHS), were ubiquitous. In the United States, rising regulation of environmental issues starting with the for-
mation of the US Environmental Protection Agency in 1971
and passing the Clean Air and Clean Water Acts through the
creation of the Comprehensive Environmental Response,
Compensation, and Liability Act (CERCLA) program; in the
1980s, the management of hazardous and toxic materials was
met with resistance and outright hostility by many businesses.
Environmental management and regulatory compliance were
cost centers to be minimized and kept distant from the core
activities of the business.

A few pioneering businesses began to question this mentality. 3M, maker of adhesives and other chemical-based products, launched its "Pollution Prevention Pays" program in
1975. The company observed that, by focusing on preventing
waste and pollution before it was created rather than manag-

ing them after the fact, it could improve efficiency and avoid compliance costs and risks. By 2015, forty years after launching the program, 3M reports that the company's actions prevented more than 2.1 million tons of pollutants from entering the environment and saved nearly $2 billion for the company. In addition, 3M reduced its energy and water use by 30% and 42%, respectively, compared to a 2005 baseline.[34]

Others such as IBM and Xerox began designing products with the environment in mind. Piggybacking on the quality renaissance of the late 1980s, Design for Environment (DfE) promised to deliver cost savings and superior products while minimizing the environmental impact of goods and services. While many firms wrestled with determining where and how to incorporate changes in their manufacturing processes, other companies realized the value of environmental stewardship, early compliance, and reduced waste streams, investing in corporate-wide DfE strategies. IBM was one of those companies, establishing a corporate-level environmentally conscious products (ECP) initiative in 1989 with a stated goal to "develop, manufacture, and market products that are safe for their intended use, efficient in their use of energy, protective of the environment, and that can be recycled or disposed of safely." Technical support was provided by a new engineering center for environmentally conscious products (ECECP), and in the years following the launch, 75% of business units had successfully incorporated DfE practices into their design processes. By 1996, IBM formalized the ECP program, requiring business units to develop and report on DfE strategies.[35]

Other organizations began to cater to a growing community of environmentally conscious consumers. The Body Shop, a company from the United Kingdom, marketed environmentally friendly beauty and health-care products to an enthusiastic customer base. Toms of Maine, founded in 1970, started selling environmentally friendly toothpaste. Throughout the 1980s, Patagonia grew rapidly from its humble beginnings in California to be a force in environmentally conscious active wear. During the same time, Ben & Jerry's grew to be a global brand selling ice cream with a strong environmental and social ethos.

By 2010, larger companies were starting to pay attention as well, investing more capital into green products and being rewarded for doing so. Research released by the Conference Board in 2015 shows that companies like GE, Philips, Siemens, Panasonic, and Toshiba saw green product aggregate revenues grow 98% between 2010 and 2013, while overall sales numbers show growth of only 15% during that same time period.[36] One of those companies, Philips, reported that green products represented 54% of total sales by 2016.[37]

Over the past two decades, more and more companies have begun to capitalize on the growing interest in the environment and sustainability. Marketers positioned their products to appeal to the "green" consumer. Facilities managers who had adopted lean management practices made the logical connection that "lean is green" and started looking earnestly for ways to minimize waste and emissions.[38] CEOs and boards of directors began to look at sustainability as a strategic issue, one that presented both risks and opportunities, and started to plan accordingly.

The Disruptive Potential of Business

Despite all this activity, the big question lingers: Are these corporate sustainability efforts significant enough to solve the problems facing our planet? Simply put, we believe the answer

is no. The efforts by business are admirable yet wholly insufficient. Simply reducing waste and curtailing emissions in manufacturing will not get the job done. The innovation imperative suggests that what is needed are not incremental changes
but disruptive innovations that upend the status quo. We need
innovative new products, services, and business models that
create value for consumers in new ways while substantially reducing environmental impacts. We also need more business
leaders with an entrepreneurial mind-set. To quote the influential Austrian economist Joseph Schumpeter, we need to
unleash the "gale of creative destruction" and transform the
economy.[39]

Most industries at some time experience a major innovation-
driven disruption. The gasoline-powered internal-combustion
engine was a major disruption to the horse-drawn carriage
market. Typewriters were replaced by personal computers.
The wristwatch industry went through a major disruption in
the 1970s as quartz technology supplanted the centuries-old
technology of mechanized watches. A similar upheaval may be
occurring again as smartwatches enter the market, transforming the watch from timekeeper to multifunctional digital-
display device. Digital technology has been a particular potent
catalyst for disruption. Amazon and its online strategy have
disrupted numerous retail categories based on a traditional
"bricks-and-mortar" strategy. Smartphones have revolution-
ized not only cellular communications but the camera market, the computing market, and the music industry, among
others. The "cloud" is disrupting the software industry, creating challenges for companies that were disrupters themselves
a mere ten to twenty years earlier.

Some of these disrupters are being hailed as "sustainability friendly." Zipcar and Uber are transforming the way we

consume automotive services. There is hope that these new business models will reduce the desire to own automobiles, decreasing manufacturing needs, increasing the utilization of existing cars, and creating opportunities to speed adoption of next-generation technologies, such as electric vehicles. Interface Carpets is a classic example of a company that redefined its market from selling something (carpets) into selling a service (carpeting services). In doing so, it created greater opportunities to design for the entire product life cycle, increasing the recyclability of its products and reducing the use of toxins and other harmful chemicals not only in carpets but in their installation as well.

Of course, disruption is not guaranteed. History is littered with innovative new technologies and businesses that never quite took hold. Hydrogen fuel cells have long been hailed as a zero-emission alternative that can meet our energy and transportation needs. While there still remains hope for a hydrogen future, the technology has advanced in fits and starts for nearly fifty years. Similarly, nuclear energy has been variously hailed as our energy savior and reviled for its radioactive byproducts and accident risks. While it has experienced significant adoption—for example, France produces 75% of its electricity using nuclear reactors[40]—further expansion remains a controversial topic around the world, especially in the wake of tragedies such as the release of radioactive material in Fukushima, Japan, after a tsunami in 2011. Even France has recently made plans to get out of the nuclear power business, passing legislation in 2015 that would reduce nuclear power to 50% of total energy produced by 2025, replaced largely by renewables and energy-efficiency measures.[41] With disruption such an uncertain proposition, how can we deduce which technologies will likely help us save the Earth and which are simply fads?

Our Argument

Value-laden pleas about what businesses should or could do cannot help us understand what they *will* do. Similarly, blind faith that markets will "figure things out" ignores the broader institutional context and the imperfections of markets. Economists are often cited for their advocacy of free markets, but they have also long pointed out the potential for market failures. Pollution is a classic example of one such failure, what is referred to as a negative externality—where individual efforts create a negative by-product that causes many to suffer. Many of our environmental resources are common pool resources—goods for which one individual's consumption reduces the availability to others, while the collective finds it difficult to exclude individuals from the pool or users or reduce consumption. Fisheries and shared rivers are common examples.

Ultimately, the extent to which businesses will innovate disruptive, sustainable technologies is determined by a complex interplay between markets and various institutional actors: innovators who champion new sustainable technologies, investors who see market opportunities in these sustainable technologies, executives who steer large organizations toward profitable and sustainable opportunities, customers who are willing to pay for these sustainable technologies, activists who pressure businesses to invest in green innovation, and governments who incentivize new sustainable technologies through regulation, taxes, and other policy levers. Each of these players influences the degree to which businesses invest in and develop sustainable technologies.

We propose a model of innovation as a system (see Figure 1). At the core is the process of innovation; the steps by which a concept is advanced into a viable product or service

FIGURE 1   A model for innovation as a system.

that disrupts existing markets or creates new markets. There are many ways of characterizing this process, but we suggest a simple four-step process from research to development to commercialization to scaling and diffusion. Each step is part of a critical path toward disruption. Not every concept will eventually scale and diffuse. In fact, most will not. The innovation process is as much a process by which concepts and technologies are winnowed with a few winners emerging in the end. Innovation is sometimes characterized as a funnel where thousands, if not millions, of ideas enter with only a handful exiting the funnel as disruptive technologies in the end.

Buffering the innovation process are two attractors: factors that help motivate action in the process. One attractor is the demand side of innovation. The demand side, or "demand pull," refers to the market incentives to innovate created by the demand for goods and technology. In other words, demand pulls the technology through the innovation process. For example, consumers can create demand pull by desiring environmentally friendly products and services. Or government can create demand pull for sustainable goods through taxes or subsidies. Or other businesses can create demand pull by demanding improvements from their suppliers, perhaps to mitigate their own risks and to avoid the ire of environmental activists.

The second attractor is the supply side of innovation, or what is often referred to as "technology push." Technology push refers to the support that is needed to drive innovation. What if innovation is not a simple Pavlovian response to a market stimulus but emerges from the genius of the innovator? This is the heart of the idea of technology push: scientists, engineers, and designers pushing the boundaries of technology and creating new goods and services that transform markets. Innovators require capital to invest in research and development and to help bring their products and services to market. Innovation arises out of a rich tapestry—what is often referred to as the innovation or entrepreneurial ecosystem. Technology push includes those resources that make up the innovation ecosystem that supports the innovation process.

Scholars have long debated the relative importance of technology push versus demand pull in driving innovation. Not surprisingly, the evidence suggests that both are critical. A broad blossoming of new technology incubators and venture funds directed to sustainable technologies will have limited impact if those technologies do not ultimately create value that is demanded in the marketplace. Similarly, the creation of market incentives—say, the creation of a carbon tax—will not lead to fundamental disruption unless there is an underlying support system to create the conditions under which innovation can flourish. Both technology push and demand pull are needed.

Surrounding our attractors are a broad set of public interveners and private intermediaries that impact the degree to which technology push and demand pull drive the innovation process. Markets are driven by a number of actors, including innovators, entrepreneurs, established businesses, suppliers, employees, investors, and consumers. Furthermore, markets do not operate in isolation. They are embedded in a broad sociopolitical system that enables and constrains their functioning. Thus, activists and NGOs, regulators and policy makers, lobbyists and legislators, global trade organizations and industry trade associations, universities and national laboratories all play a role. In concert, these market and non-market players create the conditions under which innovations either flourish or languish.

Making the Case

In organizing this book, we structure each chapter around a primary business stakeholder in the innovation process: innovators, managers, investors, and customers. In each chapter, we discuss the potential and limits of these actors to drive disruptive sustainable innovations. In doing so, we bring in other relevant stakeholders such as competitors, suppliers, policy makers, activists, and scientists. Our primary thesis is that innovation emerges out of the complex system of individuals and institutions that make up the competitive market and broader sociopolitical-economic system. For business to save the Earth, there must be systemic change that comes from these actors pushing in the right direction to create the conditions where disruptive sustainable innovations flourish.

We begin with the innovators—the creative geniuses that conceive and birth sustainable technologies. In Chapter 2, we examine the potential for innovators to push technology advancements into the marketplace. We discuss the emergence of technology and the technology s-curve and how they apply to sustainable technologies. We explore open innovation and innovation ecosystems and the role they play in driving innovators. We ask how we can broadly influence the rate and direction of innovation. Finally, we examine mechanisms such as university research and licensing, intellectual property protection, and patent policy as they apply to inventing disruptive sustainable innovations.

In Chapter 3, we turn to the manager. She is ultimately the one to bring a particular technology to market. What drives these business leaders to pioneer new sustainable technologies? We delve into the motivations of corporate executives, whether they are starting a new business or innovating within an existing business. We discuss the importance of the relationship between management and investors and the role that corporate governance plays in facilitating and constraining the pursuit of sustainable technology. We end with a discussion of the set of conditions under which there may be financial motivations for managers and their businesses to pursue sustainable technologies.

In Chapter 4, we explore whether investors, or providers of financial capital, will provide the capital to fund innovation. Innovators and managers need capital to generate and scale sustainable innovations. We examine a variety of different investor types from venture capitalists, to social impact investors, to debt providers and big banks, to the government and foundations. We examine the opportunities and limits for each investor type as they relate to sustainable innovation. We end with a discussion of how to best unlock capital to invest in disruptive sustainable technology.

In Chapter 5, we explore the demand side of innovation. In particular, the extent to which customers can drive demand for sustainable innovations. We explore the evidence that consumers are willing to pay a premium for sustainable technologies and examine the efficacy of government efforts to manipulate prices and regulate outcomes in the absence of demand. We examine a number of mechanisms that try to cultivate latent demand, including labeling schemes, product standards, and codes of conduct. Finally, we discuss the role of activists and nonprofit organizations in spurring demand.

In Chapter 6, we take a step back and look at the overall system for innovation. We return to how individual stakeholders can serve as catalysts—pushing the innovation system forward to generate the disruptive sustainable technologies that we need. We advance a comprehensive action plan for unlocking innovation for sustainability. We provide a set of specific actions that each stakeholder can take to have an impact on innovation outcomes. We end this chapter by returning to our initial question: Can business save the Earth? Synthesizing the evidence presented, we offer a realistic assessment of our prospects for innovating our way to sustainability and offer some practical guidance to improve our chances.

Chapter 2

INNOVATOR AS GENIUS

OUR SUSTAINABILITY CHALLENGE requires disruptive innovation across multiple sectors. Where will these innovative technologies come from? The "push" for technology to save the Earth can start in a laboratory or a dorm room or even inside someone's head. From the earliest concept to a nascent invention to an innovative product that changes markets, we need geniuses to help us along the way. But where do we find these geniuses? What do they need to succeed? And how much potential do they truly have to solve a problem so massive?

Mark Herrema is a classic innovator. He did not wait for government policy or big business to solve the unmet need he found in 2003. He did it himself. After reading a *Los Angeles Times* article that discussed the volume of methane produced by cows, the Princeton student and eventual founder of Newlight Technologies, got an idea—if so many materials are made of carbon, why can't we take methane otherwise lost to the air and extract the carbon to produce new goods?[1]

Producing polymers from methane emissions was not new, but producing products that could compete with traditional oil-based plastics on cost would be a breakthrough. Historically, the cost to produce polymers from methane was two to three times more than that to produce oil-based products. Newlight's breakthrough was the biocatalyst of polymers, which yielded nine times more material for the same input as previous biocatalysts.[2] The road from great idea to commercially viable product was a long one, however. Herrema and cofounder Kenton Kimmel worked several odd jobs to fund their early research, putting in fourteen to sixteen hours a day.[3] A first-generation plastic product they innovated was too brittle and easily snapped under pressure.[4] Only through repeated experimentation and failure did they make progress.

After *ten years* of research and testing, Newlight finally launched a carbon-negative AirCarbon thermoplastic that was as strong as oil-based plastics but cost significantly less. By 2014, the company had raised a total of $18.8 million in capital investments and had moved toward expanding its commercial production capacity.[5] In 2016, IKEA and Newlight entered into an agreement that allows IKEA to use Newlight's commercial-scale production facility to produce AirCarbon thermoplastic under a technology license, purchasing 50% of the material from Newlight's US plant and receiving exclusive rights to use the materials and process in its home furnishings.[6] By 2017, companies like Dell, the Body Shop, and Sprint were partnering with Newlight to offer AirCarbon products. The genius of this innovation was not only Herrema's original insight but his ability to build effective partnerships to further research, develop, and scale his solution.

The best innovators anticipate unmet needs before the rest of us experience them or know how to address them. Products like the iPhone were pathbreaking because we did not know we wanted them until they became available. That is the genius of innovators. When scientists, engineers, and designers push the boundaries of technology and create new goods and services that transform markets, they can drive groundbreaking changes in the business landscape and beyond.

But where does innovative genius come from? On occasion, such genius may be in situ. Prodigies come to mind. Mozart wrote his first symphony at the age of eight. By the young age of seventeen, he was already widely recognized for his brilliant compositions. More often, genius takes time. Economist David Galenson has written that for many, genius manifests itself only after repeated trial and error, which he refers to as the "experimental innovator." Malcolm Gladwell tells the story of the popular song "Hallelujah," originally written by the legendary musician Leonard Cohen.[7] It was raw in its original form, but Cohen manipulated the song numerous times, performing and recording radically different versions. Then a cover of the song by singer John Cale appeared on an obscure French album. This version was heard by a young rising musician, Jeff Buckley, who recorded his own version that eventually went viral, giving the song wide recognition and popularity and becoming the inspiration for numerous popular covers of the song. Only through iteration and a certain degree of happenstance did the genius manifest itself.

While this kind of genius may on occasion arise independently of circumstance, more often than not, it emerges out of a broader context of history and, sometimes fortuitous, interactions. For example, Corning's Gorilla Glass was originally pioneered as a strong, durable glass for use in automotive windshields in the 1960s, but the technology was shelved when it failed to find widespread adoption due to cost considerations. The technology sat for decades until Steve Jobs showed up in 2005 asking if Corning had a strong, break-resistant glass for use on Apple's new iPhone product. Voilà! A new product was born. By 2012, Gorilla Glass had generated \$1 billion in revenue.[8] By 2016, Gorilla Glass was in its fifth generation of design and Corning had expanded its client base to other smartphone manufacturers, like Samsung. The technology helped, in some small part, to drive a major disruption in the cellular-phone and digital-technology industries. But the lesson for us is clear. Ideas alone are not enough. Only when an innovative technology meets the right market conditions does genius reach its true potential.

Technology Emergence

So how do great ideas develop? Narratives about the development of new technologies are littered with tales of "ten-year overnight successes." We frequently hear the end of the story and maybe the beginning, but the middle is often heavily abridged. Recall one of the key inventions of the twentieth century, the "horseless" carriage, a.k.a. the automobile. The advance of engine technology in industrial applications was quickly recognized as applicable to personal transport. By 1900, dozens of automobile designs competed for dominance—the standard that others would imitate—in the same way that the basic iPhone architecture quickly came to define the smartphone market, rendering alternative designs like Palm's and Blackberry's obsolete.

In the auto industry, there were electric vehicles, steam-powered vehicles such as the Stanley Steamer, kerosene-powered engines, and, of course, gasoline-powered internal-combustion engines. At the time, it was not immediately apparent which of these power trains would come to dominate the market. It took decades for the dominant technology—the gasoline-powered internal-combustion engine—to fully control the market. For example, in 1912, 95% of the delivery trucks in New York City were electric vehicles. Electric vehicles captured 23% of the national commercial vehicle fleet before eventually disappearing completely by 1950.[9]

So why did the gasoline-powered internal-combustion engine eventually dominate? There is no simple answer. Hundreds of theories have been advanced. A particularly whimsical and possibly apocryphal explanation is that once there was a race between an electric vehicle and an internal-combustion-engine-powered car in Long Island, New York. During the early part of the twentieth century such races were common. The night before, the driver of the electric vehicle partied perhaps a little too much and showed up for the race not in top driving condition and hence lost the race. As the story goes, this was the tipping point that led to increased adoption of internal-combustion engines and eventual widespread adoption.

This story, whether true or not, highlights the path dependencies that often determine whether one technology emerges rather another. It is like the old adage that a butterfly flapping its wings in China can eventually cause a hurricane halfway around the world in the Caribbean. Small events can have a big impact on future events, including emergent technologies. The story of the QWERTY keyboard is a classic example. The standard layout of the alphabet on English-language keyboards has been around for over a century. Why are the letters placed where they are? One of the reasons was to minimize typewriter letter hammers getting caught up with one another—a common problem in early typewriters. The keyboard was designed so that letters commonly typed after one another were spaced out. While important for typewriters, this has no relevance in our digital age. Yet, the QWERTY-style keyboard persists.

The automobile story relates to what in economics is sometimes referred to as the two-arm bandit problem. Imagine you are a gambler facing two slot machines at a casino. One gives better odds of winning; in other words, it pays out more cash than the other machine on average. However, our gambler does not know which one of the machines has the better odds. A reasonable strategy for the gambler is to sample each slot machine. As he plays one machine and then the other, he begins to form an expectation that one machine is the better odds machine. Eventually, he decides to play that machine exclusively, convinced he has found the winning machine. And he may be right. But he also may have gotten lucky on the bad machine early on and formed the incorrect belief that his machine was the higher paying. Our hapless gambler may very well be playing the low-odds slot machine.

The Technology S-Curve

The two-armed bandit problem illustrates how we can get locked into an inferior technology. It is important to recognize that it is not obvious that society will naturally gravitate to the "best" technology. There are likely technologies that could yield tremendous sustainability benefits that are not being leveraged today because an incumbent technology is the dominant design. Clearly, this is the case with the electric vehicle versus the dominant internal-combustion engine. And there are certainly technologies that people are betting on to change the world that never get the kind of adoption that is required. Hydrogen fuel cells and nuclear fusion have been promoted for decades as game-changing technologies, yet they remain more aspirational than commercially widespread.

A classic observation of technology scholars is that the efficiency of a given technology usually improves along a sigmoidal curve, or "s-curve." The s-curve is a common phenom-

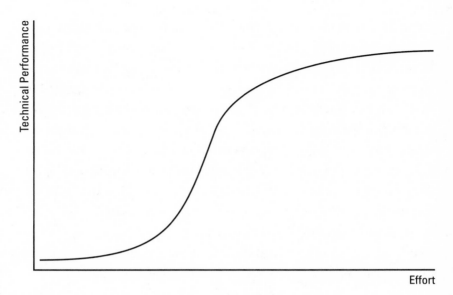

FIGURE 2   The technology s-curve.

enon observed in most technologies (see Figure 2). Early on
a new technology is typically rather inefficient. Think about
the earliest airplanes or computers—they were not very powerful and could provide only rudimentary performance with
respect to that of airplanes or computers today. As people experiment with a new technology and innovate improved versions, efficiency improves, but only slightly at first. It takes a lot
of effort to achieve even moderate improvements. With successful products, we get to a sweet spot in the learning curve
where efficiency takes off. Every unit of effort, for example,
dollars of research and development, tends to generate substantial returns.

While the s-curve is often conceived as being a function of
time, it is important to recognize that it actually unfolds based
on *effort*. The more effort put into innovating a technology,
from formal research and development to tinkering in the garage, the quicker we advance up a given technology s-curve.

However, a technology may lie fallow, not improving for years or decades if we put in no effort to innovate. Earlier in the history of the automobile it was not clear whether the electric vehicle or the gas-powered internal-combustion engine had the greatest potential. While at any point in time, we could assess which one was more efficient, it was much harder to know which one had the greatest upside. In essence, we had a two-armed bandit problem. Early experiments, in other words—effort—drove improvements in both technologies. But once attention began to shift to the internal-combustion engine, it began to outperform electric vehicles, leading to even more effort to improve the internal-combustion engine, increasing its performance advantage. Just like our gambler, eventually people stopped experimenting with electric vehicles.

Fast-forward one hundred years. We have put substantial effort into improving the internal-combustion engine. Billions of dollars have been spent to increase the performance and efficiency of these engines. We have reached the top part of the s-curve. Now every unit of effort creates only meager gains in improvement of the engine. Millions of dollars in research and development are spent to get small incremental improvements. In essence, we are tapping out the potential of today's dominant technology. However, we have electric vehicles that have lain fallow for over a half century. We are just reaching the sweet spot of the s-curve. Every unit of effort dedicated to improving the electric vehicle, such as in the battery technology, is generating substantial gains in improvement. This does not mean that setbacks do not occur. Innovation is always a noisy process with fits and starts, but the general trend is positive and increasing. Will the electric vehicle overtake the internal-combustion engine? Only time will tell, but the odds seem pretty good at this point, particularly given the efforts of major car companies. But timing is everything.

Electric engines are not a new invention, but we are just beginning to see their promise.

S-curves are critical to our understanding of technology evolution. They tell us not only about performance improvements of technology but how competition is likely to unfold and, conversely, how competition will help drive certain technologies forward or not. Early on in the s-curve, during what Cornell and Harvard professors Philip Anderson and Michael Tushman refer to as the "era of ferment," numerous companies typically jockey for position, each experimenting with different technology designs.[10] It is not uncommon to see massive entry by entrepreneurs and diversifying incumbents in an emergent industry. There were literally hundreds of auto manufacturers in the United States and abroad in the early twentieth century: such as the Studebaker Brothers, who were the leading manufacturer of horse-drawn carriages in the United States; and the Dodge Brothers, two upstart entrepreneurs who cut their teeth in the industry by supplying parts and assemblies to automakers like Ford before deciding to branch out on their own to design and manufacture automobiles.

As the number of competitors increases, competition becomes more intense, eventually causing a competitive shakeout. Numerous companies go out of business. Others merge with or are acquired by competitors. In the US auto industry, a massive competitive shakeout where hundreds of companies disappeared either through bankruptcy or acquisition resulted in the emergence of the "Big 3"—Ford, General Motors, and Chrysler. A similar dynamic played out in the market for digital music players. The new venture, Rio, was the first entrant into what was sometimes referred to as the MP3 player market. Soon incumbents such as Dell, HP, Sony, and Microsoft were offering their own versions of digital music players. But it was not until a resurgent Apple released the iPod that a dominant design emerged; a competitive shakeout resulted with numerous entrepreneurial ventures folding and many of the electronics incumbents retreating from the market. This reminds us that the company that finally achieves mass-market adoption of electric vehicles might not be the first or even second mover. For this reason, betting on specific companies rather than technological shifts is often a fool's errand.

These dynamics get even more interesting when there is a technical standard battle such as that between Blu-Ray and HD-DVD in high-definition digital video discs (DVDs). Standards battles typically emerge when there are underlying economic forces that push for a winner-take-all market—in other words, markets where a single given technology or company monopolizes the industry. We can think of the battle between electric vehicles and internal-combustion engines as a standards battle. There is value in having only one technology for a variety of reasons. One is infrastructure. Rather than build multiple networks for charging batteries and filling gas tanks, it was easier to build only one. Another is complementary technology. Software and hardware compatibility is a good example. Microsoft came to dominate the market for personal computer operating systems by allowing for easy file sharing and creating a common platform for software developers. In the case of the automobile, a vast network of suppliers arose to provide parts to the assemblers of internal-combustion engines.

One of the most powerful underlying economic forces that drive winner-take-all markets is what is referred to in economics as "network externalities," situations where the value of a good or service increases as others consume the same good or service. A classic example is the telephone. What is the value to you of being the first person to buy a telephone? Who are you going to call? The value of the telephone increases as others buy telephones. Such network externalities are ubiquitous in our modern digital era. For example, the value of Facebook to you as an individual increases as more people use the platform. It is the reason that alternatives such as MySpace struggled as Facebook grew to dominate the market. It also explains why a company like SnapChat can be a huge threat to Facebook if it can get network externalities working in its favor.

Such dynamics are important to understand as we consider the likelihood of sustainable technologies emerging and diffusing widely. Consider the market for PV cells. Currently, crystalline silicon solar cells dominate the market, representing 90% of installations. Silicon solar technology has been around for years and could be used to further scale as the demand for renewables increases, but at a great cost. While the cost to manufacture the solar cell has decreased significantly over the years, the cost of the "balance of system" (e.g., supporting hardware, labor, grid interconnection) has not changed largely because of the inflexibility of the silicon itself.[11] This cost barrier has opened the door for thin-film technologies. Cheaper to manufacture, these technologies have in the past fallen behind silicon with regard to conversion efficiency— but that is changing. First Solar has announced that it has successfully converted 22% of sunlight into energy using experimental cadmium telluride cells (commodity silicon ranges only from 16% to 18%).[12] Cadmium telluride has a theoretical maximum efficiency of 30%, well above that for silicon. The solar race continues, but it seems that if thin film costs less, is able to scale, and offers higher efficiencies, it could win out.

Open Innovation

So genius is rarely a brief flash of brilliance but more often manifests itself over time through hard work and experimentation as ideas and technologies compete for supremacy. Research by Northwestern economist Ben Jones and coauthors shows that such experimental innovation is taking longer than ever and is increasingly a team game.[13] Why? Jones argues that because the "burden of knowledge" is increasing, meaning that there is more and more research in important fields like biology, chemistry, and physics, aspiring inventors naturally take longer to master their fields and increasingly subspecialize. These additional years of work delay the great inventions and also encourage researchers to work together, both to save time and to leverage each other's expertise. Jones's work implies we should not be waiting around for the Edison or Westinghouse or Curie of sustainability. The genius we are looking for is probably a team of geniuses from different fields who have been working on the problem for a long time.

Increasingly these teams are not housed within a single organization but cross organizational boundaries through a complex web of investments, partnerships, and acquisitions. It was not always this way. Historically, large corporations approached innovation in an "ivory tower on a hill" model. After World War II, large industrial companies such as AT&T, Xerox, and IBM invested heavily in advanced research and development labs that engaged in both applied and basic science. AT&T's Bell Labs and Xerox's PARC facility in Palo Alto were leading examples of this approach to innovation. They achieved much success. Most famously, Bell Labs innovated the transistor, launching the digital age. Its scientists won Nobel Prizes and stood shoulder to shoulder with leading scientists at universities and national labs.

Fifty years later the model has evolved substantially. Corporations have largely eschewed basic research, relying on universities and national labs to bear the expense and effort. The old laboratory model was viewed as too costly. Even

when technology was innovative, companies often struggled
to move it from the lab to the market. In perhaps the most famous case, Xerox pioneered the graphical user interface and
the computer mouse at its PARC facility yet was never able to
capitalize on the technology. It took a young, intrepid entrepreneur named Steve Jobs to see the value of the technology
while visiting the PARC lab and embrace it for his upstart personal computer company, Apple.

Recognizing these challenges, companies have embraced
a collaborative strategy that has been referred to as "open innovation."[14] Today, there is a greater recognition and appre-
ciation in corporations that not all good ideas have to come
from within. They have embraced the edict, as Bill Gates once
put it, to "let a thousand flowers bloom" and work to harvest
the most attractive opportunities. This is the heart of the idea
of open innovation. "Collaborate with others" is the new mantra. Cisco Systems best reflects this new attitude. The market
leader in networking equipment, it has also been a leader in
an "acquire and develop" strategy through which it buys entrepreneurial ventures and their technology; develops it; and in-
corporates it into the company's product offerings. Cisco has
become quite adept at this strategy. Central to its strategy is
what Duke University and University of Pennsylvania Whar-
ton School professors Wes Cohen and Dan Levinthal refer to
as "absorptive capacity."[15] Cisco invests enough in internal research and development (R&D) so that its researchers remain
experts and have the capacity to absorb new knowledge outside the organization and recognize its potential.

Companies use a variety of strategies when pursuing open
innovation. R&D alliances are partnerships between two or
more organizations in which they share the costs of research
and often the intellectual property that results. Licensing is a

related strategy—a company buys the right to use the technology owned by another organization, often represented by a patent. Licensing has become a preferred way of transferring technology from university labs to corporations for commercialization. Each year universities make more than four thousand patent license agreements, bringing in about $2 billion in annual revenue.[16] Spurred on by legislative changes, most prominently the Bayh-Dole Act of 1980, universities have become a vital link in the open innovation ecosystem.

Consider the impact on corporate innovative efforts. In 2006, General Motors (GM) was investing in advancing next-generation hydrogen fuel-cell vehicles. Traditionally, this meant setting up and funding an internal team to conduct research and development. But in a world of open innovation, its choices multiplied tenfold. Should GM pursue a joint venture with a competitor such as Toyota? Should it acquire a technology pioneer such as Ballard Power Systems? Should it license from a leading university such as MIT? Ultimately, GM's hydrogen fuel-cell vehicle efforts floundered as the company fought for its life during the global recession of 2008, but the numerous paths to innovating hydrogen fuel-cell vehicles remained.

Markets for Innovation

Another approach to open innovation is corporate venture capital (CVC), which refers to corporations taking minority equity interests in entrepreneurial ventures. Sometimes they do this as a pure investment opportunity. Our own research finds, however, that the most successful CVC programs do so to gain a window on new technologies.[17] Minority ownership often gives them a seat on the board and privileged access to technology under development by the venture. The investing company may end up acquiring promising ventures it has invested in or pursue licensing agreements for the technology.

CVC highlights the increasing importance of markets for technology, sometimes referred to as markets for innovation. Markets for technology refer to the ability to buy and sell innovations across organizations. Such markets are especially prevalent when there is tight intellectual property protection, such as patents, on a technology. This helps pave the way for the buying and selling of technology through licenses and the like. Market exchanges, such as International Property Exchange International (IPXI), have arisen to specifically facilitate the buying and selling of patents and technology. IPXI allows companies to buy, sell, and hedge patent rights through the use of "unit license rights" (ULRs), which can be bought or sold like shares.[18]

Markets for innovation are particularly important for those related to sustainability. A key reason is that there is significant intellectual property being created in important domains, such as clean technology. This intellectual property helps facilitate a market for technology, where ideas can be bought and sold, contracts can be written and executed, and acquisition targets can be valued. According to the Clean Energy Patent Growth Index (CEPGI)—which tracks patents issued by the US Patent and Trademark Office for wind, hybrid/electric vehicles, fuel cells, hydroelectric, tidal/wave, geothermal, biomass/biofuels, and other clean renewable energy—more than thirty-six hundred clean-energy patents were granted to new technologies in 2014.[19]

In many segments of the broad sustainable technology market, such as renewables, development times are long and highly uncertain. Companies vary in their capacity to sustain such lengthy investments. Many entrepreneurial ventures are founded with the hope of exiting by selling the business to a larger incumbent within the industry. For example, the hope behind the sale of Nest Labs, makers of digital thermostats, to Google was that the start-up company with a promising technology would have greater financial resources and greater ability to roll products out quickly through Google's existing global network.

This interplay between entrepreneurial ventures and large incumbents evokes an age-old conundrum posed by Austrian economist Joseph Schumpeter, coiner of the phrase "the gale of creative destruction." In his early years, Schumpeter was enthralled by the impact new ventures have on the evolution of markets. It is fair to say that the hero of his capitalistic story is the intrepid entrepreneur, unleashing creative destruction on entrenched incumbents who fail to embrace innovation and change. Interestingly, Schumpeter softened his position as he aged. In the wake of World War II and the success of large-scale innovation efforts such as the Manhattan Project, Schumpeter recognized that some technologies are so complex and require such significant investment that no entrepreneur would have the wherewithal to advance them. Large organizations are sometimes necessary to advance technology.

It is interesting to think of this in the context of sustainable innovation. One can argue whether nuclear power is a sustainable technology, but what does seem clear is that two guys in a garage are unlikely to make significant advances in nuclear technology. Such advances will likely require large incumbent players, such as General Electric and Bechtel, who have the capital, the infrastructure, and the know-how to do so. In general, the necessary technical know-how likely varies greatly across sectors. In some sustainability sectors, entrepre-

neurial start-ups will be prevalent. In others, diversifying incumbents will dominate.

The Importance of Appropriability

Key to understanding these dynamics between inventors, entrepreneurs, and corporate innovators is the degree to which
each can appropriate the gains to R&D investment. Inventors,
entrepreneurs, and corporate innovators may all vary in their
ability to deliver on four tests and thus choose to specialize
in one or more stages. First, they must create more value for
consumers than alternative options, what is often referred to
as the "value test." Second, innovators must have the ability to
deliver on the value proposition, the "execution test." Third,
they need to be able to scale to meet rising demand and to displace entrenched incumbents, the "scalability test." Last, but
certainly not least, innovators need to be able to appropriate
some of their gains from their innovation to justify their effort, the "defensibility test."

What drives defensibility? Certainly, the degree to which
an innovation has what we refer to as "tight" intellectual property (IP) protection is a factor. Tight IP means that the innovation is protected from efforts by others to copy the technology. Legal IP is the most obvious example. Patents, copyrights,
and trademarks are all forms of legal IP that help companies
protect their innovations and prevent others from imitating
them, though a patent or copyright is no guarantee of successfully appropriating the gains from innovation. Countries
vary greatly in their enforcement of legal IP, especially as it relates to cross-border exchanges. Even within a country, the appropriability of legal IP can vary quite significantly. In some
industries, like pharmaceuticals and semiconductors, patents tend to confer quite a bit of protection. In others, such as

software, while patents are possible, they tend to provide less protection because it is easier for others to innovate around them—creating new software that "borrows" but does not infringe on the patent.

Ultimately, legal IP provides defensibility only to the extent that innovators are able to fight for their IP in a court of law. Many entrepreneurs have found themselves fighting larger rivals who may have impinged on their IP but who have substantially more resources to wage a legal fight should entrepreneurs assert their IP rights. For this reason, many innovators pursue other defensibility strategies. Trade secrets are one possibility: simply do not reveal the "secret sauce" that created your technology. Think of a chef with a special recipe. With some technology, it may be sufficiently complex that it would be difficult to reverse engineer. Or perhaps a technology is generated by a complicated production process that is hard for others to observe. Wes Cohen, Richard Nelson, and John Walsh found that more than 50% of all intellectual capital created is protected through trade secrets or other forms of secrecy.[20]

Another defensibility strategy is learning curves, which refer to the improvements that often result once you start playing with and producing a technology. Some firms are able to run down a learning curve before others, giving them an advantage over would-be rivals who are constantly trying to catch up. Intel has been able to maintain a technological lead in microprocessors, in part, from always being on the cutting edge with the best-in-class processors, in other words, being further along the learning curve. When Toyota launched the Prius, General Motors and others thought it was foolish. There was no way that you could make a profitable hybrid car. And they were right, at first. Toyota lost money on the early Priuses. But Toyota was moving down the learning curve and has now appropriated millions of dollars from its innovations in hybrid vehicles.

All of this is vital to consider in the context of disruptive sustainable innovations. It is not only that innovators and entrepreneurs need there to be demand for their products; they need to be able to capture some of the value created to justify their efforts. Venture capitalists have been wary of some investments in renewable energy due to the long investment horizon. Similarly, innovators may be wary of putting effort toward sustainable technologies if the payoffs are so far in the future that they will be unlikely to appropriate the gains from the effort. History is littered with successful inventors who were ultimately not able to capitalize on their inventions as others copied their ideas and outcompeted them in the marketplace.

So what can be done to create the appropriability conditions necessary to motivate innovators to expend effort on disruptive sustainable technologies? The government may play a role in its capacity of creating intellectual property rights. Some have suggested that patent policy be adjusted to provide greater benefits to innovators who create innovations that provide a significant social good. For example, those who innovate sustainable technologies will be given longer patent protection than for standard inventions (which is twenty years).[21] Alternative, sustainable technologies could be fast-tracked through the patent approval process, which typically can take up to two years in the United States.

Another way that government can help incentivize disruptive sustainable innovation is through innovation prizes, rewards given to individuals or teams who first meet some design challenge. Typically, they are awarded precommercialization, thus providing an intermediate financial incentive to an innovator who may otherwise have to wait years before the first revenues are generated. The most famous innovation prize was the original XPRIZE for space exploration. The Ansari XPRIZE competition, launched in May 1996 with $2.5 million in seed money, attracted twenty-six teams worldwide with the goal of developing a privately funded spaceship capable of safely and reliably taking people into space. By the time the award was given to Mojave Aerospace Ventures in October 2014, further investments had brought the prize amount up to $10 million. Shortly thereafter, the license for the technology was sold to Richard Branson, Virgin Galactic, and a new billion-dollar industry was born.[22]

More recently, XPRIZEs have been created in renewable energy and sustainability, including the Progressive Automotive XPRIZE for the development of safe, cost-effective fuel-efficient cars and the Water Abundance XPRIZE for energy-efficient technologies that extract fresh water from the air.[23] These prizes hold great promise as a way to help address the appropriability of challenges that innovators of sustainable technologies face.

The Role of Complementary Technologies

In most cases, for the promise of a sustainable technology to be realized requires the simultaneous innovation of complementary technologies and services. A classic example is hardware and software. Disruption in computers has often been achieved by mutually supportive innovation in both hardware and software. In fact, great advances are being made in traditional hardware products by coupling them with advances in software. The Internet of Things (IoT) is predicated on the idea of smart objects linked by software over information networks that will advance the functioning of those objects. For example, the Nest thermostat is as much a software as a hardware innovation. The software is what allows a Nest thermostat to increase efficiency and connect with users. Advances in complementary technology may be necessary to bring about a disruptive sustainable technology. One of the keys to making hydrogen fuel cells viable is finding better solutions for storing hydrogen fuel.

Manufacturing and distribution can be critical complementary services that are necessary to support a disruptive sustainable innovation. For example, advances in manufacturing may be necessary to bring an innovation to market at scale or to help lower production costs to make a technology viable in the marketplace. Recognizing the importance of advancing manufacturing to more quickly commercialize clean technologies, the US Department of Energy (DOE) launched the Clean Energy Manufacturing Initiative in 2013. The idea behind the initiative was to fund manufacturing R&D to help reduce costs associated with commercialization and grow the US cleantech economy through innovation and strategic partnerships. The program has led to advances in the manufacturing of fuel cells; batteries; solid-state lighting; and solar, wind, and other cleantech products. According to the agency's Fuel Cell Technologies Office, today more than thirty commercial products are available in the US market, and the price for high-volume automotive fuel cells has decreased 50% since 2007 partly as a result of DOE R&D funding.[24]

Alternatively, having viable distribution channels can be critical. Unilever, for example, is looking not only to change its own supply chain but also to bring about industry-wide sustainable sourcing, partnering with other companies and industry stakeholders to advocate for a broader shift in supply chain practices. Not only has the company made a commitment to source 100% of its palm oil supply from sustainably certified mills by 2020; Unilever has also partnered with the WRI to create a verification system via the WRI Global Sources Watch Platform, which is open to other companies looking to evaluate their own supply chains and potential impact on forests.[25]

Sometimes innovations need to occur upstream by suppliers before a downstream disruptive technology can reach its full potential. In our own research on the green building sector, we find that green builders require a rich array of green building suppliers, such as makers of energy-efficient toilets, installers who use natural insulation, and providers of reclaimed timber. Innovations in these supply markets help drive overall innovation and potential disruption in the building industry. Absent these suppliers, it is difficult for architects and builders to build green. Our research suggests that the absence of a robust green supplier network reduces the number of LEED-filed projects that are able to achieve certification. Business school professors Rahul Kapoor and Nathan Furr have documented the business strategies of start-ups and large companies pursuing innovations in the solar PV industry.[26] In an industry without a dominant design, the players adopt a diverse set of approaches. They find that the technology firms invest in depend heavily on what complementary assets are available. In this case it was the manufacturing equipment to produce solar modules made of either crystalline silicon, amorphous silicon, cadmium telluride, or copper indium gallium diselenide.

In all of these cases, public entities may play a role in helping innovate complementary products and services. For example, publicly funded advanced manufacturing centers have proliferated in recent years as a way to build the manufacturing capability needed to support novel technologies and to help spur economic growth in various regions. In general, there is interesting and compelling evidence that competition

is critical to a robust innovation ecosystem. Competition provides motivation for innovating; thus, the government role in
culling market power may be critical to spur innovation. Encouraging free trade and international competition and enforcing antitrust rules all help create the competitive environment necessary to spur innovation.

Complementary investments can include not only physical
capital but human capital as well. In 2012, the Batten Institute
at the University of Virginia convened the first Jefferson Innovation Summit where delegates in attendance were asked
a simple, but important question: If you were to build a more
entrepreneurial and innovative society, what would you need?
After debating many of the common factors bandied about in
such discussions—investment capital, deregulation—a group
consensus began to emerge that the single most critical factor was education. We need to train the next generation of
students both to be entrepreneurial and to have the requisite
technical skills, such as STEM (science, technology, engineering, math) education, to be able to generate the innovations
of tomorrow.

Thus, investment in public education can be a critical le-
ver to advance sustainable innovation. Talented, well-trained
individuals capable of innovation are the ultimate engine of
innovation. Arguably the historic US investment in its higher
education system has been a huge boon to its innovative output. Private foundations can also play a critical role in helping advance education and innovation. Competitions like the
Kellogg-Morgan Stanley Sustainable Investing Challenge, co-
hosted by the Northwestern University Kellogg School of Management and the Morgan Stanley Institute for Sustainable Investing, provide students a platform to present innovative new
ideas for future sustainability investment while connecting
them with industry professionals. Government-funded con-

tests like the EPA People, Prosperity and the Planet (P3) and Student Design Competition offer students grants to further develop sustainable business ideas. The cash award, mentoring, and international exposure that many of the winners receive by participating in these competitions can help develop the industry networks, identify opportunities, and hone presentation skills to successfully start up a new business venture.

Innovation Ecosystems

The open innovation philosophy, the interplay between incumbents and new entrants, and the role of complementary technologies are probably best represented in rich entrepreneurial ecosystems like Silicon Valley in the San Francisco Bay Area of California. In Silicon Valley, a rich tapestry of new ventures, established tech giants such as Google and Apple, venture capitalists, angel investors, and research institutions such as the University of California and Stanford University engage in a symbiotic exchange of talent, ideas, and capital. The results are impressive. The University of California and Stanford University ranked first and third for the total number of patents granted to universities worldwide between 2002 and 2014.[27]

An obvious question is, Where will the Silicon Valley of sustainable innovation likely be? The answer: likely Silicon Valley. Silicon Valley's ability to breed innovation coupled with some of the most aggressive climate policies in the United States has positioned the state of California as a leader in clean technology investments. In 2014, $31 billion was invested in clean technology companies worldwide—California-based companies received 17% of these investments.[28] If we look at cleantech patents, California-based inventors represented 21% of all US-based cleantech patents. This ranks California's as the sixth most innovative economy, just behind that of Germany and ahead of those of China, Taiwan, France, and the United Kingdom.[29] Clean energy technology companies such as Sunpower, Tesla, Silver Spring Networks, Enphase Energy, SolarEdge, Sun Run, and Bloom Energy were born in the Golden State. The Bay Area continues to stand at the helm of California's green innovative activity, with San Jose–Sunnyvale–Santa Clara and San Francisco–Oakland–Hayward regions receiving the highest number of green technology patents in 2015.[30]

Enamored with the success of Silicon Valley, countless municipalities and regions have attempted to build their own innovation districts and entrepreneurial ecosystems. New York, Berlin, and Stockholm are just a few of the many major cities that now have vibrant entrepreneurial ecosystems. In the United States, smaller cities, often college towns, have emerged as hotbeds of entrepreneurship: Austin, Texas; Boulder, Colorado; Raleigh-Durham, North Carolina; Charlottesville, Virginia. Increasingly, sustainable technologies, cleantech, and renewable energy are seen as possible points of emphasis in these emerging ecosystems. Boulder, a city of 105,000 residents and home to the University of Colorado, has an emerging wind cluster, including companies such as Boulder Wind Power and leading wind energy research institutions such as the National Renewable Energy Laboratory's National Wind Technology Center (NWTC).

Charlottesville, a small city of 45,000 residents and home to the University of Virginia, has seen a handful of companies emerge in the space. For example, Apex Clean Energy, founded in 2009, has become a major player in the financing and building of utility-scale wind and solar projects in the United States. Apex was the US market leader in the industry in 2015 and has brought 1,460 megawatts (MW) of wind power online over the past two years. With a pipeline of more than 12,000 MW and $90 million in recent capital raises, Apex has grown from a small start-up to a fast-growing, full-service renewable energy company comprising nearly 250 employees.[31]

Our own research into innovation in the renewable energy sector shows interesting patterns. Looking at patents filed at any of the major global patent agencies (e.g., the United States, European Union, Japan), we find that innovation in renewables, while spread around the world, tends to cluster by technology subclass. Japan and South Korea, and Asia more broadly, are known as the technology leaders in solar technology, receiving nearly 45% of patents granted between 1998 and 2010. Northern Europe is the global leader in wind patents, filing a higher percentage of wind patents than other regions of the world—49% between 1998 and 2010. The United States has led the world in biofuel research, producing 43% of biofuel patents over the twelve-year period.[32]

What might explain these patterns? While they are only speculative, one can imagine some reasonable hypotheses. Asia, Japan, and South Korea in particular have been leaders in the semiconductor industry for decades. Solar PV cells are in essence semiconductors, so it is not surprising these Asian countries would be among the leaders in filing patents for solar PVC technology. Northern Europe has been experimenting with wind technology for millennia. The central United States is known as the breadbasket of the world, given its high-efficiency farms, long being an innovator an agricultural technology and practices. It is perhaps not surprising it would be a leader in biofuel research.

Things get even more interesting when we look at patenting behavior within a country. In the United States, we see some interesting patterns emerge across regions and cities. The entrepreneurial hotbeds mentioned earlier stand out among the data: the Bay Area, New York, Boston, Austin, Boulder. But so do a number of others. Houston, Texas, is home to the US oil and gas industry and is a growing center of innovation around biofuels. Michigan, long the home of the US auto sector, is second to California in clean energy transportation patents. Santa Fe, New Mexico—located near the leading US Department of Energy Research Centers of Los Alamos National Laboratory and Sandia National Laboratories—is a leading clean energy innovator as well.

This last example highlights a common factor in innovation clusters: the collocation of research universities and/or national laboratories. The story of Silicon Valley is intricately tied to the history of Stanford University. How does a sleepy agricultural region grow to be the largest technology center in the world? Stanford University opened its doors in 1891, with the goal of producing "cultured and useful citizens." Early on the university attracted government and corporate research funds and venture capital for various start-ups in the area of radio broadcasting and then in electronics, microprocessing, medicine, and digital technology. Frederick Terman, the dean of engineering in 1925, encouraged two students to set up an electronics company in a Palo Alto garage in 1939 that would later be dubbed "the birthplace of Silicon Valley"—the two students were David Packard and William Hewlett. Terman also encouraged faculty to serve as consultants to industry and welcomed tech companies on campus to share ideas and subsidize research, practices that continue today. John Hennessey, Stanford's tenth president, who completed his term in 2016, was a board member for both Google and Cisco and a successful entrepreneur in his own right, cofounding MIPS Computer Systems, now MIPS Technologies, which designs microprocessors. Companies like Google, Yahoo, eBay, LinkedIn, and E*Trade are all linked to Stanford.[33]

In general, universities and national laboratories provide an incredible feedstock into the innovation ecosystem. According to the US Patent Office, the top 250 US universities were granted 4,632 patents in 2012,[34] or 38% of all patents issued to US applicants in that year.[35] More critically, universities educate the next generation of entrepreneurs. Google and Yahoo were started by Stanford alumni. A 2012 Stanford study estimates that the revenues generated from companies formed by Stanford entrepreneurs were $2.7 trillion annually, creating 5.4 million jobs since the 1930s.[36] An MIT study released in 2015 claims that MIT alumni have "been among the founders of at least 30,000 currently active companies." The study also estimates that 4.6 million individuals work at these companies, which generate annual global revenues of $1.9 trillion.[37]

Most interesting, these entrepreneurs tend to collocate near their alma maters. In Stanford's case, 25% of the graduating entrepreneurs after 1990 built their companies within twenty miles of the university.[38] In MIT's case, 31% of the alumni ventures were started in Massachusetts; 8% were built within Cambridge, which represents the highest share of MIT alumni companies in the United States.[39] These results are not limited to MIT and Stanford. A study of ours of the alumni of the University of Virginia (UVA), a public university that receives funds from the Commonwealth of Virginia, found similar results. UVA alumni ventures have created 371,000 jobs in the commonwealth, producing $395 billion in calculated revenue and spending $279 billion per year.[40]

National laboratories, funded by the federal government, can provide a similar feedstock into innovation ecosystems. The Bay Area is home not only to Stanford University and the University of California at Berkeley but also to a number of national labs: Lawrence Berkeley National Laboratory, Lawrence Livermore National Laboratory, SLAC National Accelerator Laboratory, and Sandia National Laboratories. MIT and Harvard have had an indelible impact on the greater Boston entrepreneurial ecosystem, but they have been aided by labs such as the Brookhaven National Laboratory and the Princeton Plasma Physics Laboratory in the northeastern United States. Santa Fe is a hotbed of renewable energy innovation and is home to a cluster of national laboratories. In each case, federally funded R&D helped advance the underlying science and technology that ultimately became a driver to downstream commercialization efforts.

All in all, while the impacts of innovation may be global, its genesis tends to be local. We need rich, entrepreneurial ecosystems focused on developing disruptive sustainable technologies. This lends credence to the claims of former New York City mayor Michael Bloomberg and others that cities have a critical role to play in addressing climate change and other sustainability challenges. Not only can they reduce their own impact; they can serve as hotbeds of innovative activity that can fuel the sustainable technologies of tomorrow.

Innovator as Genius Redux

Innovation is not a solitary act. Genius may on occasion be in situ, but it typically manifests itself through the complex interplay of numerous institutions and actors who encourage and support innovation: In universities and national labs where disruptive technologies are hatched. In communities and coffee houses where creative people bump into each other and ideas are shared and advanced. In incubators and accelerators where ideas become prototypes. In corporate research centers where researchers, working with entrepreneurial ventures, take ideas from prototype to launch. In legislatures where policies are set that determine the rules for patents or who create innovation prizes to spur creativity. Together these players push technology forward with the hopeful result of a stroke of innovative genius.

In this chapter, we identify a number of opportunities to create the conditions under which such genius may emerge: Investing by the federal government in basic research in sustainable technologies through national laboratories and sponsored university research. Changing intellectual property laws to favor technologies that provide sustainability benefits. Creating advanced manufacturing facilities and programs to help scale promising sustainable technologies. Fostering vibrant local entrepreneurial ecosystems that target sustainability by cities and municipalities. Reforming regulations to ensure that they do not stifle new technology that may not fit existing regulatory regimes. Offering of large cash prizes by the government or foundations for innovative sustainable technologies. Leveraging the research capabilities and the entrepreneurial spirit of university faculty, students, and alumni to address sustainable technologies. Educating primary, secondary, and college students in STEM fields so they can be the sustainability geniuses of tomorrow.

Together, these prescriptions can be a powerful catalyst for energizing our innovation system toward disruptive sustainable technology. Unfortunately, they are not enough. As we have highlighted throughout this chapter, there are no guarantees that the most socially beneficial innovation will win out in the marketplace. Conceiving and developing sustainable technologies are only half the battle. Those technologies need to compete with others that are perhaps proceeding up their own s-curves. For a sustainable technology to be truly disruptive, it needs to create value for consumers that exceeds alternatives and to do so in a way that creates value for the innovator and his partners in commercializing and scaling the technology.

It is tempting to think that a genius is being born today somewhere who will invent the solution to our sustainability challenge. And while perhaps that baby born today will one day invent a new electric engine or an advanced solar cell with the potential to transform the transportation or energy sectors, she will need a lot of help along the way. While she might do her work inside a university, in a federal lab, or maybe at a start-up company or corporate R&D office, the success of her idea will be determined not just by technical merit but by whether a broader constellation of managers, investors, and ultimately consumers see merit in her idea and deliver and scale it in the marketplace. She may be the genius we have been waiting for, but that alone will not be enough to save the Earth.

Chapter 3

MANAGER AS HERO

FOR A NEW INNOVATION to address our sustainability challenge, it needs to be commercially viable. A sustainable technology that is not adopted contributes little to sustainability. Testing viability typically happens inside a company. Building successful business models and creating a robust product road map are not easy. The sustainability space is littered with great ideas that never saw the light of day because no businessperson could figure out a way to sell and profit from them. To save the Earth, we will also need expert managers to recognize great ideas, turn them into products, and figure out how to sell to the mass market.

Consider Elon Musk. Musk did not set out to save the Earth. Raised in South Africa, he moved to Canada to attend Queen's University and then to the United States to pursue bachelor's degrees in economics and physics at the University of Pennsylvania. He dropped out of grad school at Stanford at the height of the Internet boom and started a new venture called Zip2, a web software company that offered city "guides" and was later acquired by Compaq for $307 million. Shortly after this sale he cofounded X.com, an online financial services company that eventually became PayPal.

Fresh off his success with PayPal, he turned his attention to two lifelong obsessions, space exploration and renewable energy, founding SpaceX in 2002 and helping launch Tesla Motors in 2003 as an investor and chairman of the board. In October 2008, Tesla, facing bankruptcy, turned to Musk, naming him CEO with the hopes that he could turn around the company and change its fortunes. And turn around the company he did. Tesla's Model S has been one of the best-selling electric vehicles worldwide. The release of the more affordable Model 3 has opened the door to more consumer-friendly ranges (two hundred–plus miles) and price points ($35,000 for the base model), pushing electric vehicles further into the mainstream with some help from the growing electric charging-station network—more than fourteen thousand charging stations and close to thirty-seven thousand charging outlets located across the United States in 2016.[1]

In 2010, the company went public and has grown exponentially ever since. There is no doubt that companies like Tesla, Nissan (the Leaf), and Chevy (the Volt) are disrupting the automobile market, forcing other companies to play—BMW, Audi, Cadillac, Chrysler, Fiat, Ford, Hyundai, Kia, Mercedes, Mitsubishi, Porsche, Toyota, Volkswagen, and Volvo now offer electric or hybrid models—especially in light of more stringent fuel-efficiency regulations on the horizon. But Tesla's long-term vision and growth were more strategic and focused not only on electric vehicles but also on storage and sustainable sourcing.

Tesla Energy was launched in March 2015, offering "a suite of batteries for homes, businesses, and utilities fostering a clean energy ecosystem and helping wean the world off fossil fuels."[2] The only part missing now was the renewable source.

So in 2016, Tesla acquired SolarCity Corp, a full-service solar provider and a company that Musk was already invested in, helping his cousins start the venture in 2006. With this acquisition, the company "would be the world's only vertically integrated energy company offering end-to-end clean energy products to [its] customers."[3] These steps have led many to predict that Musk will be the business leader who single-handedly transforms the energy and automobile industries, weaning them off fossil fuels.

Elon Musk, Bill Gates, Jack Welch, Warren Buffett, Richard Branson, Steve Jobs, Mark Zuckerberg: leading entrepreneurs and business executives who are among the most famous people on Earth. They are rock stars of the twenty-first century. They are frequent guest speakers on the lecture circuit. Best-selling books are written by them. Best-selling books are written *about* them. They are profiled in major motion pictures (for example, *The Social Network* or *Steve Jobs*). More often than not, they are celebrated for their vision, their tenacity, and most important, their success—not only for amassing huge fortunes but also for their ability to create new markets and products that impact our lives.

When we first posed the question, "Can business save the Earth?," perhaps you thought about these leaders of some of the most famous companies in the world. Can these "heroes in the corner office" solve our seemingly intractable sustainability challenges through their ingenuity, adept management, and force of personality? Many are certainly trying and bringing their companies along with them. Richard Branson of Virgin Enterprises has invested time and money into several environmental initiatives, cofounding the Carbon War Room, a nonprofit that seeks to identify market barriers, bring together investors, and accelerate the introduction of sustainable solutions. Building on Branson's commitment to sustainability, Virgin America announced in December 2015 the acquisition of ten new state-of-the-art aircraft engines that are 20% more fuel and carbon efficient than those of its current fleet (already 15% more efficient than competitors').

A charismatic business leader, passionate about the environment, can make sustainability a priority in his organization. A new generation of CEO activists is taking a public stand on important economic and social issues that are not obviously connected to short-term profits.[4] Many of those executives are using their bully pulpit to impact public policy and attitudes toward sustainability. Jim Rogers of Duke Energy has long supported sensible environmental regulations. He was among the only business leaders in this industry to support efforts for a cap-and-trade system in the 1990s to reduce sulfur dioxide emissions, even testifying before Congress on the issue. In the 2000s, he launched the Climate Action Partnership to push for a cap-and-trade system on greenhouse gas (GHG) emissions and was a key player in the Waxman-Markey Bill in the US Congress in 2009, which narrowly passed the House of Representatives but eventually died in the Senate.[5] But Rogers's activism has encouraged other business leaders to advocate for policies that will encourage sustainability while at the same time pursue internal efforts to green their own organizations.

This kind of activism might seem puzzling to those who are familiar only with the conventional wisdom that the purpose of business is to make profits and nothing else. The truth is that the espoused mission of a business is rarely to simply maximize shareholder returns. Mission statements are often far more expansive and inspirational. Google defines its mission as to "organize the world's information and make it universally accessible and useful." Starbucks is not just about making a better cup of coffee but rather about using its network of twenty-three thousand stores in more than seventy countries (2016) to improve the very communities it serves, including investing in the education and employment of young adults in those communities. Microsoft touts that "our mission is to empower every person and every organization on the planet to achieve more."[6]

Mission statements are not empty rhetoric. They articulate aspirations. They define the markets in which a business will participate. They express values and outline how the organization intends to compete. Founders and chief executives, as the leaders of their enterprises, help set and shape their missions and can wield great influence on whether an organization will pursue innovative sustainable products, services, production processes, and business models. Many have made it their mission to address sustainability. Should we expect them to succeed?

Corporate Governance and Greening

Even the most passionate "green" executives are ultimately constrained by the owners of their businesses. In many businesses, the owners are not only those who founded or led the enterprise but those who provided capital for the business, such as venture capitalists or other investors. Technically, owners maintain residual rights of control—meaning that, unless specified contractually, they get to determine the actions and directions of the organization, often referred to as corporate governance. In practice, this includes the approval of any major strategic decisions and, most important, the responsibility for hiring and firing the chief executive.

The separation of ownership from management is a relatively recent phenomenon in the long history of markets. Only since the beginning of the twentieth century has there been a substantial shift away from owner-operators to hired professional managers. Despite the proliferation of professional managers, about 90% of US businesses are still family owned. This includes everything from your mom-and-pop small businesses to large private, family-run corporations such as Mars Inc., makers of M&Ms and other candies. While large public companies capture the public's imagination, the vast majority of organizations remain owner operated. According to the US Census Bureau, in 2012 there were 6.6 million US companies, of which less than 6,000 were publicly traded.[7]

Owner-entrepreneurs are an interesting class of such businesses. The initial founder of a business (an entrepreneur) may maintain control of her venture for many years both from a leadership perspective, serving as president or CEO, and from an owner perspective, being the largest shareholder in the enterprise. There are a number of interesting examples of owner-entrepreneurs leading their enterprise to embrace sustainability. Patagonia founder Yvon Chouinard has long incorporated sustainability objectives into Patagonia's strategic plan and arguably has left profits on the table to do so. Famously, he has constrained the growth of the enterprise, even going so far to state, "Don't buy this shirt!" in one notorious advertising campaign.

Recent research suggests that these so-called green entrepreneurs may differ from traditional entrepreneurs. In our own research, we have found evidence that entrepreneur entrants into the emerging industry for green-building supplies in the United States were far more likely to be motivated by protecting the environment than were diversifying incumbents—existing building suppliers who started offering green product lines. Diversifying incumbents generally were responding to a market opportunity. Green entrepreneurs were often on a social mission, while also hoping to make a profit when doing so.

A particular challenge for these green entrepreneurs is what happens as the business scales. Will they be able to maintain control? To finance growth in their business, entrepreneurs will often give up ownership stakes to venture capitalists and other investors. In many cases, these investors will end up taking a controlling interest in the firm. For the venture capitalists, the end game is to either sell the firm or launch an IPO (initial public offering), usually after a relatively short period (five to ten years). Often, in either case, the result is the venture becoming a publicly traded company.

All of this raises the prospect of an owner-entrepreneur eventually losing control of her business. Steve Jobs was famously forced out of Apple in 1985 by Apple's CEO John Sculley with the support of Apple's board of directors after the two clashed on strategy and philosophy. Sculley was brought in as CEO in 1983 after serving as president at Pepsi-Cola. Jobs did not return to the role of CEO for twelve years. Jeffrey Hollender, cofounder of Seventh Generation, a pioneer of green cleaning products, stepped down in 2009 as CEO and was replaced by Chuck Maniscalco, a former PepsiCo executive. Maniscalco was brought on to scale the company further, charged with increasing company revenues from $150 million to $1 billion. Hollender continued to serve on the board and as the face of the company before being ousted by board members one year later in 2010 because of differences of opinion on the long-term vision for the company.[8]

To avoid just these sorts of problems, some entrepreneur founders take measures to retain control. Some have simply resisted going public in the first place. For example, Patagonia, Menards, and Mars all remain privately held enterprises under the control of their founder (or family members). They have been able to fund their growth either through retained earnings, debt, or other arrangements that allow them to maintain a majority ownership stake in their business. Some entrepreneurs have structured their IPOs so that they maintain effective control over the company even after going public. Google founders Larry Page and Sergey Brin maintain control of the company through a dual-class stock share structure,[9] which gives them majority voting rights despite owning roughly only 12% of the company's equity.[10] They have used this power to invest in a diverse array of technologies, including renewable energy and driverless vehicles, seemingly far afield from their core business of Internet search. Fortunately for Page and Brin, investors are so eager to own a stake in Google, they are willing to give up control to do so.

Sometimes owner-entrepreneurs voluntarily give up control. Ben Cohen and Jerry Greenfield of Vermont ice-cream maker Ben & Jerry's are famous as much for their progressive social stances as for their quality ice cream. In the face of declining performance and outside calls for new leadership, they chose to sell their business to the consumer goods conglomerate Unilever in 2001. Ben & Jerry's went public as a subsidiary of Unilever but retained some independence by creating a separate board of directors charged with maintaining the company's social mission and protecting the brand's integrity. Cohen and Greenfield were given spots on the board and preferred stock.[11] While Unilever managed Ben & Jerry's largely as an independent subsidiary and maintained many of its signature programs, there were many who felt that Ben & Jerry's unique culture and emphasis on social issues such as sustainability had suffered as a result of the acquisition. Cohen and Greenfield would later regret selling, reportedly citing concerns about the company's shift in focus away from social responsibility.[12] Ben & Jerry's is not alone. Toms of Maine was sold to Colgate-Palmolive in 2006. The Body Shop was sold to L'Oréal in the same year. Burt's Bees was sold to Clorox in 2007. In all of these cases, the founders have been criticized for "selling out."[13]

To avoid such situations and to allow organizations to maintain their founding values regardless of ownership, legislatures have created a number of new organizational forms. Benefit corporations, or B Corporations, are the most prominent among them. B Corporations bake into their corporate charters explicit profit *and* social objectives. These objectives are explicit, and management is required to measure and report on them in disclosures to owners. As of July 2015, twenty-eight states in the United States had passed legislation authorizing benefit corporations. Other similar examples of new legal forms of organization include low-profit limited-liability companies (L3Cs) and the flexible-purpose corporation authorized in California.

B Corporations and their ilk are relatively recent innovations but are gaining traction. As of January 2017, more than two thousand companies had certified as B Corporations through the nonprofit B Lab.[14] Patagonia and Method have reorganized as benefit corporations. Such a reorganization does not necessarily change any of the current values or initiatives of the firms, but it provides a layer of protection if the business is ever acquired by another entity that may have different values or strategic directions. In 2015, Etsy, the online craft bazaar, became the first benefit corporation to go public, trading on the Nasdaq stock market.

It is important to note that all corporations have the opportunity to advance social objectives. The often-heard bromide that companies have a "fiduciary duty" to maximize shareholder returns is actually factually incorrect from a legal standpoint. Fiduciary duty refers to the responsibility of managers and boards of directors to inform owners of their intent. If a manager wishes to give 15% of profits away to charity, she can do so as long as she keeps owners informed of her plan. If the owners disagree, they can either disallow the action or, if needed, remove the manager from the organization. In fact, publicly traded companies routinely give money to charity through corporate philanthropic efforts. In 2015, the top twenty most charitable Fortune 500 companies donated $3.5 billion.[15] The real question is whether the owners of a publicly traded corporation, the shareholders, will allow the pursuit of sustainability objectives by the business's managers.

The Tyranny of Shareholders

There are approximately forty-three thousand publicly traded companies worldwide.[16] While relatively small in number, publicly traded firms loom large in public awareness and impact. Walmart and McDonald's together employ a total of four million people, ranking third and fourth behind the US Department of Defense and the People's Liberation Army of China in total employment.[17] According to the Forbes Global 2000 list, publicly traded companies account for $35 trillion in revenue,[18] or 47% of 2015 global GDP.[19] They are a big presence and have a big impact on the environment. One study released in 2010 by the United Nations estimated that the top three thousand publicly traded companies were responsible for one-third of the environmental damage (including cost externalities) caused by human activity.[20]

While a privately held company may be able to pursue far-flung objectives when given the green light by owners passionate about sustainability, a leader at a publicly traded company is typically far more constrained. This manifests itself most obviously in the pressure on CEOs to deliver quarterly earnings in line with financial analysts' forecasts. Repeated failure to deliver on those expectations can lead to a CEO's removal. There are numerous cautionary tales of executives who reached too far, pulling their organization down a path that led to the company floundering and to the executive being removed by shareholders. Sir John Browne of BP was forced to retire early after a scandalous personal story broke. However, contributing to the willingness of the board to remove him was a sense that the company had placed too much emphasis on its sustainability initiatives at the expense of its core oil business, leading to a decrease in profits and, ironically, to a chronic lack of attention on safety issues within its traditional business units.

The tyranny of quarterly earnings has led some to argue that we should give managers more discretion in leading their organizations—to free them from the demands of capital markets. Many CEOs argue that pressure from financial analysts leads them to forgo long-term investments in favor of short-term actions that boost the stock price. CEO Lars Sorensen at Norvo Nordisk, a global pharmaceutical company, explained some of these challenges in an interview in 2015 with the *Harvard Business Review*: "As a U.S. CEO, you cannot ignore responsibilities to shareholders. You can say, I'm going to increase shareholder value over 15 years, so hang on with me—it's going to be a little tight the next couple of years. But unless you have block ownership and can convince shareholders they're going to be richer in 15 years than if they sell the stock now, then someone will walk in with a successful offer to buy the company, because you're not performing. The only way to change this, if society wants to change it, is to see pension funds behave differently with their investments."[21]

Using the same logic, some executives have argued that they wish to make long-term capital investments that will help improve the bottom line and advance sustainability, but they are fearful to do so because capital markets will punish them for raising costs in the short run. Bill George, former CEO of Medtronic, described in an interview in December 2013 that the challenge is that "the stock market, particularly the New York Stock Exchange, is shorter term than ever and we have this new class of investor activists who are very, very aggressively involved, looking for short-term gains: Dollar or two a share. Come in, make a quick hit, move."[22] Exacerbating this mentality is the massive growth in executive compensation tied to the company's stock price through options and bonuses. According to one report released by the Conference Board, *CEO and Executive Compensation Practices: 2015 Edition*, stock awards accounted for 42% of CEO pay for S&P 500 companies.[23] The *Wall Street Journal* reported CEO cash compensation to be at 37% in 2015, based on research conducted by the Hay Group.[24] Coupled with shorter CEO tenures, on average 5.2 years, down from 10.3 in 1990, CEOs are very wary to take any action that will negatively impact the stock price in the short run.

Surveys confirm the perceived importance of shareholder interest and short-term profits versus longer-term investment in initiatives that benefit the greater population. A survey by McKinsey & Company of one thousand board members and top executives around the world found that 86% of respondents feel that taking a longer-term strategy approach when making decisions would have a positive impact on company performance but feel beholden to stakeholder's desire for short-term gains.[25] Some CEOs, however, like Paul Polman of Unilever, are charging forward with corporate responsibility initiatives not because of return on investment (ROI) but because of a core belief in the responsibility of the business to be a good steward. Tim Cook, the CEO of Apple, when asked about the company's energy sustainability programs, and moving forward only those things that were profitable, replied, "When we work on making our devices accessible by the blind, I don't consider the bloody ROI." It was the same thing for environmental issues, worker safety, and other areas that do not have an immediate profit. The company does "a lot of things for reasons besides profit motive. We want to leave the world better than we found it."[26]

Is Short Termism the Problem?

There has recently been increasing concern about whether the pressure of reporting quarterly earnings has negatively influenced public companies' willingness to invest in cutting-edge sustainable technologies. BlackRock CEO Larry Fink famously wrote in a 2016 letter that "many companies continue to engage in practices that may undermine their ability to invest in the future." Partly in an effort to remove quarterly earnings pressure, there has been a trend to privatization, largely led by private-equity concerns. Between 1996 and 2012, the total number of companies publicly traded in the United States fell from eight thousand to forty-one hundred with roughly half of this differential due to delistings.[27] Some of these were motivated, at least in part, to address sustainability concerns. Most famously, private-equity giant KKR, along with TPG Capital and Goldman Sachs Capital Partners, took TXU Corporation (renamed Energy Holdings Group) private in 2007 for $45 billion, which was at the time the largest leveraged buyout (LBO) in history. TXU was one of the most profitable electric utility companies in the country, serving more than three million people. As part of the deal, investors agreed to abandon eight of TXU's previously planned eleven new coal-fired power plants and invest millions of dollars over the next five years in conservation and energy-efficiency initiatives.[28] The deal was hailed by environmentalists as a huge win, avoiding millions of tons of carbon emissions otherwise released annually.[29]

Will privatization ultimately lead to better environmental outcomes? Does giving managers more discretion increase the likelihood that they will invest in sustainable technologies? It is not clear. Private ownership could just as likely lead to worse outcomes. For every Patagonia, there is a Koch Industries—one of the largest privately held companies in the United States, heavily invested in fossil fuels and extractive industries such as mining, and a vocal and active lobbyist against a progressive environmental agenda. Private-equity firms have been criticized for their tendency to seek short turnarounds of struggling public companies by bringing them public and cutting expenses through layoffs and curtailing of long-term investment such as R&D. Will managers in these companies be more likely to invest in sustainable technologies?

There is a reason that economists often cite agency issues that arise when managers are given too much discretion. Agency refers to the possibility that managers will act in their own best interest at the expense of the company and, in particular, the owners. In 2002, long-term Tyco chief executive Dennis Kozlowski made the news for his lavish lifestyle at the company's expense, including a $2 million week-long birthday party for his wife on the Italian island of Sardinia. Even more troubling, Kozlowski and his chief lieutenant were convicted in 2005 of stealing $150 million from Tyco and making $430 million off the value of the company stock that they artificially inflated. Infamously, Enron executive Kenneth Lay oversaw a massive fraud. Their activities led to the collapse of the company and the loss of billions of dollars by investors. The nightly news was peppered with stories about small-time shareholders such as Tom Padgett, a sixty-three-year old senior lab technician, who was laid off from Enron right before his planned retirement and lost $700,000 in retirement savings.[30]

It seems to be wishful thinking that most managers will, out of the goodness of their hearts, transform businesses to be sustainable if given more license. A rich corporate governance literature bemoans the discretion that managers do have. Through deep board interlocks, where executives appoint one another to each other's boards, executives can inoculate themselves from pressures from their shareholders. Combined with the use of stock-based incentives and compliant board compensation committees, the result has been a massive increase in executive pay. In the United States, executive compensation has increased 46% since 2009 and 940% since 1978. The CEO annual compensation at the top 350 companies was $15.5 million in 2015.[31]

Of course, not all executives are out to simply enrich themselves. Some executives may leverage their discretion to make long-term investments in sustainable technologies. Interestingly, some have cited these types of sustainability-oriented investments as just the type of vanity projects that corporate governance activists rage against. Savvy executives know how to justify sustainable investments in the language of corporate finance—that such expenses have a positive return on investment or simply that it "pays to be green." A cynic may say that these are yet again a manifestation of the principal-agent problem. Charismatic executives, who want to look good to their friends, family, and adoring public, pursue vanity projects around sustainability. The cynic may see no difference between a CEO's sustainability initiative and his or her justification for a corporate jet or a $10,000 business dinner.

Is Green Business Also Good Business?

Even a well-intentioned executive with board approval cannot drive sustainable innovation on his own. The charismatic leader who singularly overcomes all obstacles is a popular myth. These tales make for great business school case studies but offer very little insight into how things actually work. To be successful, sustainable innovation takes collaboration and buy-in from a wide number of stakeholders. Businesses need capital and the support of suppliers and employees to commercialize and scale innovations. A charismatic executive who is passionate about sustainability needs to convince many others and secure commitment of their time and resources.

Personal charisma ultimately does not create value on its own, and businesses need to create and capture value to survive. This typically requires products and services whose value exceeds the cost of production. Our colleague Ed Freeman has said, "We need red blood cells to live, the same way a business needs profits to live. But the purpose of life is more than to make red blood cells, the same way the purpose of business is more than simply to generate profits."[32] No one would argue that producing red blood cells is the purpose of your body, but they are most definitely needed to survive. Similarly, the purpose of business is not to produce profits, but businesses need profits to survive. Profits flow to the residual claimants of the enterprise, especially their owners, who in turn provide capital and other resources to the business. Profits can ultimately be reinvested in the enterprise—what are referred to as retained earnings—to help fund growth and innovation efforts.

Even nonprofits need to generate an inflow of funds (either in the form of revenues like tuition at colleges or through philanthropic donations) that equal their cost of production. Otherwise, they will eventually wither and die from a lack of funds to fuel their efforts. Scaling, in particular, is a struggle for most nonprofits. If their costs grow linearly with their effort, they will need to grow their funds proportionately. For example, to double their impact, many nonprofits would need to double their intake of donations. Thus, any expansion of impact requires excess funds with respect to the status quo. While these excess funds are not profits per se, they are critical to the growth of nonprofits.

This discussion begs the question: What evidence do we have that sustainable innovation is profitable or generates excess funds? Fortunately, there is much evidence to support the argument that green business can be good business. Books are full of anecdotes of how businesses have realized significant financial gains by investing in sustainability. In *Green to Gold*, Dan Esty and Andrew Winston looked at green "wave riders," a list of fifty companies ranked by their favorable environmental footprints, and found that their stock prices outperformed the S&P 500 and FTSE 100 indexes year to year between 1998 and 2008.[33]

A vast academic literature also provides empirical support for the thesis that it pays to be green. Large data sets have been constructed, measuring firm environmental behavior and financial performance across a wide number of industries and over many years. While the results are not unequivocal, there is evidence suggestive of a positive correlation between environmental performance and financial performance. In our own work, we find that, on average, a 10% decrease in a company's toxic emissions as reported in the US Environmental Protection Agency's Toxic Release Inventory—a database of toxic emissions from US manufacturing facilities—results in an average 3% increase in a firm's financial performance as measured by return on assets.[34] Another study suggests that a 10% reduction in emissions could result in a $34 million increase in market value.[35]

Many questions remain. How to best measure environmental performance is a particularly perplexing challenge. Environmental performance includes factors from emissions of greenhouse gases, to the production of solid waste, to the recyclability of company products at the end of life. Measuring and aggregating these various factors has itself inspired a vast literature. Life-cycle analysis (LCA) has arisen as an approach to measure the net environmental burden of a product or service over its entire life cycle from extraction of raw supplies, to manufacturing, energy use, product use, and ultimately to disposal or recycling. The weighting of various environmental factors is ultimately subjective and hinges on decisions such as whether clean air or clean water is valued more.

Measuring financial performance is surprisingly not much easier. Accounting measures such as net income or return on assets are notoriously influenced by the vagaries of annual reporting. Market-based measures such as Tobin's q (the market value of a firm over the replacement value of its assets) rely on the accuracy of capital markets to correctly forecast future earnings of the firm and price them accordingly. Absent from most analyses, typically, are natural experiments that allow one to observe the counterfactual of what would happen to financial performance if a firm did or did not pursue a specific sustainability initiative. These measurement challenges are more than academic debates. CEOs need to use data and analysis to convince stakeholders to support green initiatives. Without reliable measures of what green even means and how to connect these efforts to the bottom line, this case gets harder to make.

Ultimately, we do not think there will ever be perfect measures. Yet there is too much accumulated evidence to argue firms should *never* invest in sustainability. Similarly, it is highly unlikely that *all* investments in sustainability have a positive financial return. Certainly, there is no empirical support for this latter claim. At some point, eliminating waste or reducing the use of certain resources will be too expensive to justify financially. A much better question is, "Under what conditions does it pay to be green?" Or stated another way, "When is green business good business?"

Green Is Lean

Sustainability makes financial sense whenever it either increases people's willingness to pay for a product or service or lowers the cost of providing the good or service. The spread between willingness to pay and cost is what creates profits.[36] There are definitely situations where there is sufficient demand for green products and services among customers who are willing to pay a price premium for sustainability. The Body Shop, Toms of Maine, and Patagonia all have successfully tapped the growing segment of eco-friendly consumers. The market for Teslas and Toyota Priuses is, at least in part, driven by the green inclinations of their buyers. The question of what drives demand for sustainable technologies is important enough and complex enough that we dedicate an entire chapter to this topic (Chapter 5).

Another reason that green business can be good business is that it may placate concerned stakeholders who would otherwise hinder the creation and capture of value. For example, environmental activists can put significant pressure on businesses to invest in sustainability through protests, boycotts, and other forms of civil disobedience. Each of these actions by activists can command valuable managerial attention and ultimately result in real costs to the business. Government can place significant pressure as well, not only through the obvious mechanism of regulation but also through its control of access to critical resources such as federal land and water, as a major purchaser of goods and services, and through its funding of research and development.

Many times, it is simply for reasons of efficiency that managers go green. Waste is waste. Green is lean. There is compelling evidence for this proposition. We have found a correlation between those firms who adopt lean management practices and those who have lower toxic emissions.[37] Anecdotal evidence abounds of companies who have cut expenses and identified new streams of revenue by turning their attention to their waste streams. For example, General Motors generated $2.5 billion in revenue from 2007 to 2010 through various recycling efforts and continues to bring in $1 billion annually from by-products leaving GM facilities to be recycled.[38] Numerous analyses have found that companies who adopted more-efficient LED lighting in their facilities often paid back their capital investment in as little as one year, creating significant financial savings for the firm. With LED prices rapidly declining, paybacks will be even more favorable. And since new lighting technologies are lasting longer (as much as fifty thousand hours, or almost six years in facilities operating 24-7), these investments are continuing to pay back long after capital expenses are covered.

Economists are typically perplexed by such cost-saving opportunities. They question why, if these "win-win" investments are so abundant, they have not been already pursued. Could managers really be so blind to miss out on these seemingly obvious opportunities? This brings to mind the old joke about an economics professor and her student walking down the street and happening upon a $100 bill lying on the sidewalk. The student bends down to pick up the bill when the professor stops him. "Clearly, the $100 cannot exist. For if it did, someone would have already picked it up!"

The fact is that businesses do walk by $100 bills on the sidewalk. Otherwise, there would be no need for innovation or R&D. The question is, When do they discover them? A rich body of literature looks at the role of information in driving the discovery of profitable opportunities. Researchers have found, in particular, that managers often fail to recognize potential cost savings from environmental initiatives. In one such study, Andy King at Dartmouth found that managers at electronics manufacturers in Massachusetts were typically disposing of chemical by-products in a sluice that ran down the center of the factory.[39] At the end of the pipe, the chemicals were treated and disposed of according to EPA regulations. When the Toxic Use and Release Act (TURA) was passed in Massachusetts in 1989, these factories were required to account for the toxic chemicals coming out of the pipe. The regulation forced them to analyze their waste stream. What many of them discovered was with simple changes to their processes, they could not only reduce the waste being produced; they could generate significant cost savings through reduced material use and end-of-pipe effluent handling. Until compelled by regulation, they had never thought about analyzing their waste stream, but once they turned their attention to it, they discovered cost-saving opportunities.

Green Employment Savings

Another way that green business can be good business is by reducing the costs of labor, in other words, human capital. Businesses are ultimately made up of people. To the extent that employees care about the environment, they might compel business leadership to pursue green initiatives. Employees may be willing to work for less pay or work harder for a company they believe in, increasing labor efficiency and lowering labor costs. A 2015 study finds that 66% of young millennials (ages eighteen to twenty-four) would be willing to take a pay cut to work for a responsible company.[40]

Going green may also help with hiring and retention by providing intrinsic benefits to employees. Recent studies find that scientists and researchers in corporations receive as much value from intrinsic incentives as they do from extrinsic benefits such as pay.[41] Investing in sustainability may allow employers to attract the best and brightest candidate to their organizations. Retaining them results in lower employee turnover, reducing employment costs in sourcing and onboarding talent. The same 2015 study suggests that 82% of young millennials take into account a company's corporate responsibility report when deciding whether to take a job.[42]

Surprisingly, there is scant empirical evidence of employee cost savings from green initiatives, in large part, because there have been very few studies of this relationship. This is due in part to the challenges of measuring and testing employee cost savings. It is likely that the employment benefits of going green vary greatly across industries. One important consideration is labor costs as a percentage of total costs. For certain labor-intensive industries, employment incentives can have a material impact on the business. Consider Starbucks. The company has one of the lowest employee turnover rates in an otherwise high-turnover industry—12% in 2013 compared to more than 70% for the larger hospitality industry.[43] Arguably, its environmental initiatives help attract and retain talented baristas in its shops. And with training estimated to be around $3,000 for each new barista, the company has also rolled out some impressive employee benefits, including tuition assistance.[44] This is critical since dedicated employees are such an important aspect of a positive customer experience at Starbucks.

Employment savings are not necessarily material in all businesses. While every employer wants to attract talented, dedicated individuals, the costs of going green may not be sufficiently offset by the employment benefits. The employment payoffs to go green are tied to labor markets and the macroeconomic job environment. Anecdotally, in our years teaching college students, not surprisingly there appears to be a correlation between the selectivity of students and the business cycle. When times are good, students can afford to be picky, demanding to work for sustainability-friendly businesses. Yet they may be willing to work for a "brown" firm if jobs are tight.

Greening the Supply Chain

Many businesses sell to other businesses and might have some degree of influence to green the entire supply chain, not simply their own organization. Enterprise involves a web of interactions with suppliers, retailers, distributors, and alliance partners. To what extent could these business partners incentivize managers to support sustainable innovation, in other words, to green the supply chain? In some cases, downstream buyers can motivate change up the supply chain. The demand for sustainable products and services filters up to early-stage producers and component manufactures who go green to meet the demands of downstream business-to-business (B2B) purchasers.

For retailers, most of the environmental impact of their products happens within the supply chain outside the narrow confines of the company. An estimated 97% of the environmental impact of consumer goods comes from product manufacturing, raw materials, and transportation.[45] To address the sustainability across its supply chain, Walmart, the largest retail company with a whopping $485 billion in revenue in 2014, launched the "Sustainability Index" in 2009 to measure the environmental impact of Walmart products.[46] So far, Walmart has applied the index to seven hundred categories across the business.[47] A *Time* magazine article marking the fiftieth anniversary of Walmart praises the company for its unprecedented partnership and coordination of the company with the suppliers.[48] Walmart wants to eliminate twenty million metric tons of GHG emissions from the supply chain and claims to have eliminated 7.575 million metric tons (MMT) of GHG by the end of 2013, expecting to eliminate 18 MMT of GHG emissions by the end of 2015 through various projects that it has undertaken.[49]

Home Depot, the world's largest home-improvement retailer, has been implementing a wood-purchasing policy since 1999 to address the destruction of ecologically important and nonrenewable rain forests in its supply chain. The company gives preferential treatment to Forest Stewardship Council (FSC)–certified sustainable wood. Today, Home Depot sells very little wood coming from the rain forests, and much of its wood comes from certified sustainable sources. Working closely with manufacturers and suppliers, Home Depot has become the largest seller of FSC-certified wood products in the United States and helped the largest number of vendors to transition to selling FSC-certified wood.[50]

These initiatives can be powerful drivers of change. Interestingly, they all go back to the incentives for those downstream companies to require environmental compliance. What motivates downstream companies to push sustainability? In Home Depot's case, it is responding to consumer demand for sustainable timber. In Walmart's case, it is trying to provide information to consumers while minimizing its own costs. In this way, it is passing the costs of sustainability up the supply chain.

Some of the most intriguing efficiency gains from going green may be achieved with a broader coordination of the supply chain. Engineers, arguing that industrial systems should resemble natural systems, have advanced the field of industrial ecology. In particular, they argue that industrial symbiosis can be achieved by turning waste flows into by-products that are feedstocks for other industrial processes. The most famous example of such a closed-loop system is the town of Kalundborg, Denmark. Located seventy-five miles west of Copenhagen, Kalundborg industrial park has evolved into an ecosystem of companies where one company depends on the other for materials and energy inputs. It works like this: Treated wastewater from one refinery is used as cooling water for a power station; the refinery's surplus gas is also used by the power station as an input; excess heat and steam is used by other companies and neighboring homes for heating and other uses; and fly ash produced by the power station is used for cement manufacturing and road building. [51]

These industrial eco-parks hold great potential, so why don't they arise more often? Several attempts have been made in the United States and Europe, but few of these attempts have been successful.[52] Part of the problem is that coordination remains difficult. A vast literature in economics looks at the transaction costs that arise when trying to coordinate exchanges of goods and services. The colocation typically required by otherwise independent companies in parks such as Kalundborg opens up the partners in the exchange to holdup problems where one party demands better contractual conditions before continuing to provide or accept a by-product feed stream. For example, these types of coordination problems could be a reason why there has been little progress on the hydrogen economy some scientists advocate. The creation, transport, and use of hydrogen create a series of complicated exchange relationships that likely raise transaction costs.

The Problem of Low-Hanging Fruit

Overall, the perspective that green pays holds much promise. Numerous firms have experienced significant cost savings by addressing wastes and inefficiencies. Additional opportunities for sustainable innovations that lower costs are likely. However, there are reasonable concerns that all of this is simply "low-hanging fruit"—easily grabbed efficiency gains that quickly dissipate. Efficiency gains may drive substantial sustainable innovation, but it is unclear whether these are likely to go far enough to address the sizable challenges that we face. Ultimately, there must be decreasing returns to environmental investment.

As illustrated in Figure 3, at some point, the cost savings will not offset the expense. If we assume that there are decreasing returns to environmental investments (the value line) and increasing costs to continuing environmental investment, the spread between value and cost will ultimately turn negative. Likely the cost of eliminating the very last bit of pollution or environmental impact from a product will be very costly (hence the increasing cost curve).

Auden Schendler, climate activist and vice president of sus-

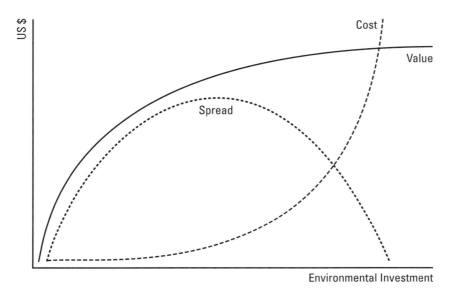

FIGURE 3   Value-cost spread and decreasing returns.

tainability at an Aspen ski resort, in his book *Getting Green Done,* provides wonderful examples of how at every turn his efforts to make the ski resort a sustainable enterprise was met with resistance and challenge. When he first arrived in Aspen, he honed in on energy-efficient lighting as a quick win for his sustainability efforts. Armed with spreadsheets demonstrating the positive return on investment for installing efficient light-ing, he quickly ran into resistance. To the hotel manager, the new lights were too yellow. To the security manager, they were not bright enough. While Auden was ultimately successful in making the change and many others, he highlights that go-ing green is challenging and real trade-offs are quickly faced.

Numerous CEOs have reflected on the challenges of push-ing forward with more sustainable innovation after initial rounds of success. In a recent sustainability survey among more than one thousand top executives in 103 countries, a clear frustration is visible: a struggle to make a business case for sustainable action and significant market failure to tackle the global challenges. Many expressed their feelings that they have already done as much as possible given the existing market constraints. CEOs confided about being stuck in "pilot paralysis"—small-scale, one-off projects with incremental impact. They expressed their unease about the conflict between the need for fundamental business performance and scaling up sustainable actions.[53]

Manager as Hero Redux

If incremental change is difficult, what are the prospects for game-changing innovation? What are the opportunities for generating fundamentally disruptive innovations that reshape markets and significantly reduce environmental impacts? Ironically, the very fact that incremental change is difficult may create the conditions under which disruption is more likely. Entrepreneurship scholars have observed that entrepreneurs often emerge to solve a market failure, to meet some consumer need that is not currently being satisfied in the market. Jeff York and Venkat Venkataraman argue that our sustainability challenges create numerous market failures, thus creating the incentives for entrepreneurs to enter the market to solve those problems.[54]

The good news is that disruption does not require every company to invest in sustainability. Only a handful of successes are needed to displace intransient incumbents. Economist Joseph Schumpeter introduced the idea of "creative destruction," in which he theorized that new, entrepreneurial firms innovate—in the form of a new product, technology, or service or a new form of organization—which gives them a distinct advantage over incumbents within the industry. Ultimately, this leads the entrepreneurial ventures to become leaders in the industry, replacing the incumbents.[55] Indeed, it has been found that existing dominant firms often fail because new technology-based firms bring creative disruption to the marketplace.[56] Even when incumbents survive, they often follow the blueprint of the new entrants and help make the new technologies mainstream:[57] "out with the old, in with the new," as the saying goes.

In reality, creative destruction rarely follows the relatively clear Schumpeterian path. The innovation system determines whether the innovation will thrive or die a premature death. One innovation may depend on other relevant innovations in the supply chain or complementary industries. For example, solar and wind power generation technology will become truly ubiquitous when cheap storage technology becomes widely available. Hydrogen fuel may not take off without a breakthrough in cleaner and cheaper production of hydrogen.

Another important factor may be competing technologies. If fossil fuel continues to be widely available at a cheaper price, renewables will have a hard time gaining ground. An available support structure for new technology is also critical in many industries. If a network of reliable recharging stations is not available, electric cars will not become mainstream even if they become comparable to internal-combustion vehicles in performance and value. The problem is that considerable uncertainties are often involved with new technologies and the investment needed for the support structure can be huge, which may be infeasible without the existence of a sizable market, resulting in a classic chicken-and-egg situation.

Consider Tesla's case. It was not the eco-conscious but rather the rich-car types whom early designs targeted. This allowed the company to design a car that looked cool and offered the bells and whistles desired by this type of consumer, in addition to being electric. Years later, building on this brand recognition, Tesla introduced a more cost-competitive electric model for the general population. The Model 3, priced at just over $30,000, received 180,000 orders in the first twenty-four hours of its March 2016 introduction. Many economists see price competitiveness with gasoline designs as the tipping point for electric cars, suggesting that this could come as early as the year 2022. By the year 2040, electric cars are forecast to represent as much as 35% of total car sales.[58] Unlike the industry's foray into electric cars in the 1990s, the market forces today are moving in unison, generating the consumer demand needed to propel electric technologies forward.

Leadership does matter, but business managers operate in a constrained environment. They must be responsive to their equity holders, they must be cognizant of their customers, they must raise capital for investment, they must convince suppliers and others to partner, and they must understand the demands of activists and government. The purpose of business is not to make profits; it is to create value. However, the ability to create value is contingent on the business creating profits, or it will disappear. Can we simply rely on heroic business leaders to lead the way? No. We must create the conditions under which such leaders can thrive and survive: the Fords, the Jobses, the Musks. The key for our heroic managers is to find partners willing to invest in disruptive sustainable technologies that ultimately provide value where the willingness of customers to pay exceeds the costs. In the next chapter, we discuss these investing partners, the gamblers placing bets on uncertain and nascent technologies.

Chapter 4

INVESTOR AS VISIONARY

EVEN THE BEST INNOVATIONS typically do not immediately generate returns. They require investment up front to develop the concept or technology into a product, test out different variations, and educate customers. New product launches are risky and many fail. So who would be willing to invest in unproven sustainable technologies? It turns out that many investors are lining up to pour money into them. And we will need even more of them if we hope to significantly change the rate and direction of sustainable innovation. Investors will come in different shapes and sizes, but the key requirement for success is the ability to see something in the idea, the team, or the market that no one else does. Even the best ideas will never work without adequate investment.

Consider David Friedberg and Siraj Khaliq, two friends with an idea but not enough money. The two former "Googlers" recognized that climate change and the growing global population were putting a significant strain on the agriculture industry. According to the Food and Agriculture Organization of the United Nations, the demand for food around the world will be 60% greater in 2050 than in 2006.[1] Farmers needed help. Topsoil depletion was impacting farm productivity and leading to other environmental impacts such as increased use of nitrogen and water as farmers worked to keep up with demand. Friedberg and Khaliq saw an opportunity to provide the information needed to farmers looking to operate their farms more sustainably. Founded in 2006, WeatherBill offered weather data and insurance to a number of sectors, focusing inclusively on agriculture. The company changed its name to the Climate Corporation in 2011.

But even with a compelling sustainable business idea, they could not get very far without capital. In stepped venture capitalist Vinod Khosla and his namesake, Khosla Ventures. Khosla met with CEO David Friedberg early in the development of their "software as a service" decision support tool that would help farmers monitor crop health and land use to optimize operations and maximize crop yield. Khosla challenged him to think bigger, to become the "Bloomberg for Farmers." The tool was initially envisioned as a small side project, but the company invested significant capital and staff into the tool development and created a more functional and stable tool that was well received in the market. With Khosla's encouragement, Friedman sold the company to Monsanto two years later for $1.1 billion.[2]

A key ingredient to launching any business idea inside a new or existing organization is money. Businesses need capital for investment: to conduct research and development, to build prototypes, and to expand capacity. From the professor in the lab seeking federal grants to pioneer in a new technology to the CEO looking for venture capital (VC) to launch a new product, sustainable businesses require investors willing to fund them. The cash can be used to pay for lab equipment or production facilities, pay scientists and engineers, or launch brands and advertising campaigns. Where does this money come from? Investors. It is rare for a business to be able to grow and scale without infusions of outside capital. Even a billionaire like Elon Musk requires capital beyond his own means to pursue his most audacious business ideas.

Investors come in many shapes and sizes. For the intrepid entrepreneur, friends and family are often the first stop for financial support. Angel investors and venture capitalists can provide a valuable bridge from nascent venture to product launch and revenue generation to profitability. Private-equity and public-capital markets may provide finances to help a venture scale. Investors need not be private financiers. Public entities and nonprofits are also valued investors. Through grants and direct investment, governments finance innovation. Similarly, private foundations are increasingly investing in innovative activities.

Of course, investors typically expect some return on their invested money. For public funders, the return may simply be the creation of new technologies that help drive economic growth or address pressing social needs such as climate change. For most private funders, the expected return is specifically a financial return. More formally, the key question is can investors expect a financial return on their invested funds that exceeds the returns they are likely to receive from an alternative investment of similar risk? Risk is an important concept to investors. Given alternative opportunities to invest their capital, what is the risk and likely reward of investing in sustainable technologies? Even if an investor believes that it "pays to be green" in an absolute sense, that may not be sufficient to motivate investment if the risk assumed is sufficiently large. The greater the risk, the greater the expected return for investors.

Investing in disruptive technology, in general, is risky and is likely doubly so in the case of sustainable technologies. The payoffs associated with disruptive sustainable technologies are likely distant and depend on future states of the world that involve the interaction of consumers, government and public policy, and other nonbusiness stakeholders. The upshot is that sustainable technology requires patient capital willing to take risk.

Private Funding of Sustainable Innovation

To what extent can we expect some bold investors to step into the fray and invest in sustainable technologies? Venture capitalists are a primary vehicle for investing in promising technology start-ups. For our purposes, we include under the label "venture capital" formal venture capital funds as well as related investors such as angel investors and private-equity funds. Are venture capitalists likely to invest in sustainable innovation? In 2015, venture capitalists invested over $59 billion in start-up companies within the United States.[3] Cleantech investments represented roughly $1.3 billion of 2015 venture capital investments, earning cleantech a spot in the top ten sectors with more mature industries such as biotech, industrial/energy, and IT services.[4] Vinod Kholsa, a cofounder of Sun Microsystems and famous for his early-stage investments in companies such as web portal Excite and optical networking company Cerent, launched his own sustainability fund with over $1 billion in capital in 2004. From 2004 to 2014, clean energy venture capital investments more than doubled.[5]

Despite the interest by venture investors, there are also numerous challenges across different kinds of green technology. While there are socially oriented venture funds and angel investors, the vast majority of venture capitalists behave like tra-

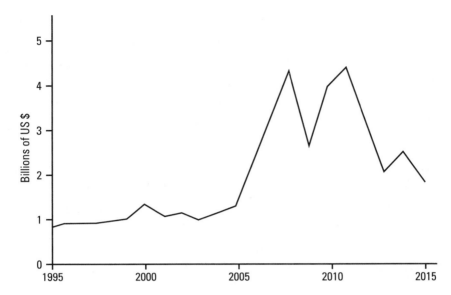

FIGURE 4   US venture capital investment in cleantech, 1995–2016. Source: PricewaterhouseCoopers / National Venture Capital Association MoneyTree Report, data Thomson Reuters.

ditional investors; they are most interested in the financial return on the capital invested. Sustainable technologies have some unique attributes that make them both an intriguing and a limited opportunity for venture investors. While venture capitalists have been very active in investing in nascent green technologies, there is concern that many of these investments are long-term, high-risk development projects that do not well fit a venture-capital or private-equity model, where returns are generally expected within five to ten years. As documented in a 2016 report from MIT, venture-capital investments in cleantech have performed poorly, with software cleantech companies being the only bright spot.[6] Figure 4 shows the growth and decline in cleantech investment by venture capitalists since 2004.

Of course, venture capital is not the only way innovators fund the development of their technologies. Established publicly traded companies like General Electric raise money through the public-equity markets to fund internal research, development, and commercialization. Due to the scale of these companies, investments in sustainable technologies can have significant impact. But just as venture capitalists weigh the return on investment from funding new start-ups with risky technology, corporations face the same uncertainty regarding their internal investments. As discussed previously, there is some correlational evidence that public markets value green initiatives, but it cannot certainly be assumed that the markets will respond favorably to *all* green investments. So established public companies contemplating significant initiatives in sustainability need to carefully consider the "response from the street," Wall Street.

Investors are becoming more sophisticated about how they select sustainable companies for their portfolios. Early efforts focused on simple screens for "sin industries" like tobacco and firearms. But these screens face significant challenges. First, it would be potentially more valuable for investors to know which firms within a given industry, such as mining, had the most sustainable business practices rather than the coarse distinctions between "good" and "bad" industries. Second, even within "sin" industries it might be socially beneficial to identify companies making sustainable investments. The key to these environmental, social, and governance (ESG) ratings is to provide investors with transparency about environment, social, and corporate governance performance of a publicly traded company. The thinking is that if the information is provided transparently, socially conscious investors will "vote" with their dollars and allocate them to the most sustainable enterprises.

While trillions of dollars have been invested under the banner of social investing, the ratings that underlie this allocation are controversial. Our prior work has documented that the numerous ESG raters frequently disagree with each other about whether the same company is a sustainability leader or laggard. This is driven partly by having different methodologies but also likely due to simple measurement error. Equally worrying, it does not appear that the ratings have any predictive power, as we would expect traditional stock ratings to possess. We found no evidence that high social ratings were associated with fewer corporate scandals in the future.[7]

Recently, there has been considerable consolidation in the ratings industry, and the professionals who work in this industry are making significant efforts to improve the transparency of their methodologies and quality of the ratings. These improvements should help aid the flow of capital to the firms that are actually sustainable, not just the ones that have figured out how to game a given ratings system. Fewer such firms could also mean greater consensus over measurement approaches, which would be a positive thing from our perspective.

Despite the concern over the quality of ESG ratings for investors, firms seem to pay attention to them. We have found evidence that firms that receive poor environmental ratings subsequently improve their environmental performance. There are mixed results on how investors react to firms being added or dropped from various social indices based on these ratings, but discussions with corporate executives indicate that the performance on ESG ratings is something to which senior management pays attention.[8]

Relatedly, a broad class of social investors, increasingly called impact investors, have emerged and hold particular promise for incentivizing sustainable innovation. Social and impact investment is simply another form of traditional investing to the extent that it is simply about creating bottom-line benefits by recognizing the profit potential in going green. In fact, some funds tout this as their *main* benefit: by looking at social impact, one can uncover hidden financial value. Far more interesting is the situation in which investors are willing to accept slightly lower returns for environmental goods. According to the Forum for Sustainable and Responsible Investment, sustainable, responsible, and impact investment accounted for $8.72 trillion, or one-fifth of total investment under professional management. Since 2014, sustainable investing has grown 33%.[9] Stanford and the University of California System announced moves to divest from coal-producing companies in 2014 and 2015, respectively, due to environmental concerns but also future financial uncertainties and risk.[10]

Or consider the Sisters of Saint Dominic, a Catholic nunnery located in Caldwell, New Jersey. Included in their 1995 vision statement is a commitment to the environment: "We resist the ongoing devastation of our planet by a contemplative scrutiny of our use/abuse of Earth's gifts."[11] In 2011, the Sisters released an official corporate stance on climate change that includes "supporting the development of sustainable energies and advocating for more environmentally responsible corporate policies and practices."[12]

To this end, the Sisters of Saint Dominic have successfully used minority equity stakes to bring proxy vote battles to numerous companies, asking them to adopt the Ceres Principles. Ceres, created in 1989 by a group of investors following the *Exxon Valdez* oil spill in Alaska, is an advocacy group for sustainable business practices, working with investors, companies, and public-interest groups toward a more sustainable economy. The Ceres Principles are a ten-point code of corporate conduct that includes commitments to energy conservation, sustainable use of natural resources, reduction and proper disposal of wastes, protection of workers and communities, and systematic reporting of progress.[13] Hard to ignore, many firms will negotiate with the Sisters and often acquiesce to their demands to sign the Ceres pledge.

Ultimately, the question is whether this particular class of social investor lowers the cost of capital for businesses and makes it easier to be green. There may not now be a significant enough pool of capital from this source to motivate businesses to invest in sustainable technology. Helping fill the void not covered by venture capitalists and social investors, a number of specialized financial ventures have stepped up in recent years to fund sustainable innovation. Sunfunder is one such company that is thinking outside the box to help pave the way for renewable energy. While utilities and other industry stakeholders in developed countries fight over regulation, pricing, and grid standardization, Sunfunder is working to bring solar power directly to regions that have never had access to reliable energy sources, essentially leapfrogging fossil fuels altogether. Through its Solar Empowerment Fund, Sunfunder is able to provide entrepreneurial solar companies short-term loans to help establish and scale operations in these hard-to-reach areas. According to the International Energy Agency, there are 1.2 billion people in the world who do not have access to electricity. That is a significant market (17% of total population) and one that has sparked the interest of private investors and more than a dozen solar start-up companies. The US government has provided Sunfunder a $15 million loan through the Overseas Private Investment Corporation (OPIC), a financing arm of the federal government, to support such innovative challenging development projects.

To date, Sunfunder reports funding $13.8 million in solar projects, providing more than two million people with clean and affordable energy.[14] Sunfunder is just one of several renewable-energy financing organizations around the world of-

fering small companies with big ideas the opportunity to play
in the energy market and providing investors a funding vehicle to influence global change. Government incentives for renewable-energy projects, such as those offered in the United
States, have helped to further entice investments in renewable
energy. So far, the bets being made by early investors seem to
be paying off as renewable-energy pricing continues to fall
and investments in solar and wind projects surpass fossil-fuel
investments (2 to 1 in 2015).[15]

Debt Financing of Sustainable Innovation

Debt providers, such as large commercial banks and local savings and loan organizations, are another important class of
investors. How do debt providers such as large banks differ
from equity capital providers in their tolerance for sustainable innovation? Many large banks follow the Equator Principles, which are guidelines for evaluating and managing environmental and social risks for projects that they finance. In
the United States, Bank of America, JP Morgan Chase, Citi-
group, and Wells Fargo are Equator Principles financial institutions.[16] The International Finance Corporation (IFC), part
of the World Bank Group, has also issued Environmental and
Social Performance Standards that provide the expectations
of its clients in managing such risks.[17] These financial institutions look at sustainability from an insurance perspective.
What are the potential downside risks of a project due to environmental impacts such as climate change? They are interested in managing these risks by identifying and, to the extent
possible, ameliorating the environmental hazards.

Mobilization of debt capital in the form of bonds is becoming an increasingly important part of the financing solution for a low-carbon economy. Bonds are particularly suitable

for investment in low-carbon projects because of their very high initial cost and long-term low operational cost and stable revenue.[18] Green bonds are specially labeled bonds created with a purpose to fund projects that have positive environmental and/or climate benefits.[19] Green bonds were created in the early 2000s by a group of development banks.[20] Starting from almost nothing in 2007, global green bond investment reached $11 billion in 2013 and tripled within a year to $36.6 billion in 2014.[21] Even though formal green bonds consist of a fraction of the currently unlabeled "climate-themed" bond market,[22] green bonds provide a credible liquid option for investors to invest in green companies. Green bonds are usually no different from traditional bonds except that the issuers of green bonds pledge to use the funds for purposes that will benefit the environment, the criteria are made public, and investors and issuers make a promise to report about how the money is spent.[23]

Demand for green bonds has been very high with significant oversubscription.[24] In the last ten years, investment grew almost fivefold and cumulative investment reached more than half a trillion dollars.[25] The $1 billion Green Bond released by the IFC in February 2013 sold out within an hour.[26] Globally, more than $13 trillion—almost 22% of professionally managed assets—have ESG as one of the selection criteria.[27] The fact that investors are becoming more and more concerned about climate change is reflected in the global investor statement on climate change. In 2009 when it was first published, 181 investment institutions managing $13 trillion in assets urged for a global agreement to tackle climate change with drastic measures such as 50% to 80% emissions reduction by 2050.[28] In 2014, support for such action reached 367 investors representing more than $24 trillion in assets. The investors are increasingly worried about the economic risks associated with climate change and their impact on investment.[29] Investors representing more than $3 trillion have declared a specific interest in investing in bonds focused on climate change solutions.[30]

Investment is not limited to US and European issuers. In the last few years, well-known companies in India, South Korea, China, and Taiwan have issued green bonds worth hundreds of millions of dollars. China is of special interest for the growth of green bonds. In fact, of the half-trillion-dollar climate-themed global bond market, China is the largest issuing country with bonds worth $164 billion; the United Kingdom is in second place with bonds worth less than $60 billion. This is mainly due to the bond issued by the China Railway Corp, one of the largest builders of rail infrastructure in the world.[31] In 2013, the State Council of China decided to promote the corporate green bond market as part of its twelfth five-year plan for the country.[32] The Chinese government is planning to spend $275 billion in the next few years just to clean up the air of Chinese cities, notorious for their deteriorating air quality.[33]

A large part of the success of green bonds is driven by demand for investment in emerging and developing economies. First, these countries face disproportionately higher risk from climate change and its impact on water, agriculture, food, disease, and poverty.[34] Second, many of these countries lack well-developed infrastructures. This creates an opportunity to leapfrog browner technologies and to be considerably greener from the start. Most of the investment financed by green bonds is for physical infrastructure, but these investments can help spur innovative new start-ups both to build and supply that infrastructure. While there are concerns about transparency and potential greenwashing with green bonds, especially in the absence of a well-defined universal standard and established certifying organizations,[35] green bonds hold promise as an alternative financing opportunity for sustainable technologies.

Public Financing of Innovation

Private investors are not the only source of funds for sustainable investment. Governments can be a significant investor in sustainable innovation, spending over a trillion dollars a year in research programs globally. In the United States, the National Science Foundation (NSF), the National Institutes of Health (NIH), the DOE, and even the Department of Defense (DoD), provide funds that help advance science and technology, sometimes in a direction toward sustainable innovations. However, with only $6 billion assigned to clean-energy technology programs government-wide in 2015[36]—about 5% of the $113 billion total federal R&D funding for that year[37]— many have argued that this number is woefully inadequate to spur the scale of sustainable innovation needed. In general, federal R&D spending has been reduced by 10% in the last ten years under budgetary pressure from the US Congress.[38] With the election of the Trump administration, prospects for increased funding for research in sustainable technologies seem dim.

More promising, potentially, are programs like the federal R&D tax credit to help incentivize research investment. While a boon to large incumbent players who spend millions, if not billions, on research, the R&D credit has limited impact on entrepreneurs who often have no net income and, therefore, are already not paying corporate taxes. The Small Business Innovation Research (SBIR) program is an alternative vehicle that targets nascent entrepreneurs. The SBIR program provides grants to small businesses involved in scientific R&D.

Funding is tied to federal agencies whose extramural R&D budgets exceed $100 million. These agencies are required to give at least 3.2% of their budgets to small business research efforts. While this is clearly impactful in some cases, critics point to a number of deficiencies in the program. Similar to many federal grants, SBIR grants are awarded on a competitive basis, so hundreds of companies are competing for the same funds, potentially costing the small businesses time and money and in the end, perhaps no grant. The application paperwork and follow-up documentation can be unwieldy and overly strict. Many in the scientific community, while supportive of the program to help bring more innovative technologies to market, fear that the money being given to small businesses is taking away from national laboratories and other federal institutions.[39]

More controversially, the US government decided to directly fund entrepreneurial ventures in 2005 as a way to help them scale. The Energy Policy Act of 2005 authorized the energy loan program and was designed to support and help bring to market new clean-energy technologies. The program is probably most famous for underwriting Solyndra Inc., a maker of solar panels founded in 2004. At the time, prices for polysilicon were rising, which provided an opening for the company, who planned to build panels using more expensive materials than polysilicon but offering cheaper installation. In 2009, the company was granted a government-guaranteed loan for $535 million to help it scale production. Meanwhile, several market shifts were working against Solyndra—natural gas prices were falling, prices for polysilicon were also falling, and Chinese companies were outcompeting American companies in the panel market. Despite several warnings about the company's future, including an independent audit by PricewaterhouseCoopers, DOE restructured the loan in 2011, allowing some investors to agree to give the company an additional $75 million in financing. By August 2011, the company had filed for bankruptcy.[40] Findings of the Congressional Energy and Commerce Committee pointed to a lack of DOE oversight of the company's financials as well as questionable acts in the restructuring of the loan.[41]

Solyndra was not alone. Abound Solar Manufacturing was also an early recipient of DOE funding. Just two years after being granted a $400 million guaranteed loan, the company declared bankruptcy. Another prominent public investment failure during this time was Fisker. After receiving a DOE-guaranteed loan for $529 million, the company unveiled its first luxury electric car in 2008. After missing production deadlines, falling significantly behind in orders, numerous recalls and consumer complaints, and failure to pay on the loan, DOE ceased funding at $192 million and the company filed for bankruptcy.[42] Many used these failures as an opportunity to discredit the clean-energy loan program, despite the many companies that benefited from the assistance and were thriving, including Tesla. Lost on many commentators was the high risk of providing capital to entrepreneurial ventures. The fact is that the majority of entrepreneurial ventures fail to provide a positive return on investment.

Public Funding of Infrastructure

Where the government may have its biggest impact on disruptive sustainable innovation is investment in infrastructure. For example, in the high-tech industry, much has been written about platform technologies. The Internet is a prime example. The government-funded Internet spurred a revolution in communication and exchange and has disrupted a broad range of industries from media to software to retail. In this way, the Internet served as a platform technology for other innovations. Similarly, mobile computing driven by the diffusion of smartphones, such as Apple's iPhone and Google's Android operating system, has facilitated the innovation of numerous disruptive products and services such as Uber in the livery business.

In the case of sustainable innovations, physical infrastructure can be a critical catalyst. Electrical infrastructure is an obvious case. The promise of distributed renewable energy, such as residential and commercial solar and wind energy, depends on a smart grid that can regulate loads and pricing with thousands, if not millions, of electricity generators. Over the last several years there has been a collective movement across the United States toward a more flexible grid, with states and utilities taking different approaches to encouraging distributed generation. Today, customers generating electricity on-site are unable to directly sell excess electricity to other customers. However, by the end of 2016, forty-one states, Washington D.C., and four territories were providing renewable credits and reduced rates via net metering and other compensation programs. These programs are open to solar and other technologies such as wind, geothermal, and fuel cells. As the programs mature and customer generation grows, utilities are reviewing and adjusting program pricing structures to strike a balance between electrical grid needs and customer benefits.[43] Continued investment in updating the electrical infrastructure in the United States and other countries allowing new distributed energy technologies to feed into the grid could go a long way to increasing the market share of renewable energy.

Similarly, the viability of distributed renewable energy also depends on the availability of reliable and inexpensive storage options. Given the current regionalized and intermittent nature of renewable energy, storage solutions seem to be critical for increasing dependence on sources such as sun and wind, dispensing excess energy to the grid during cloudy or low wind periods. Yet some scientists are now suggesting that renewables could supply all of the US energy needs without the need for massive storage if the national grid more efficiently transmitted the energy from the regionalized renewable sources across the broader United States.[44] But even in this scenario some level of energy storage will likely be incorporated into the system to help with grid flexibility and climate uncertainties. However, such grid expansion and rebuilding, as well as changes needed to the regulatory system and the manner in which utilities operate and predict demand, would take years to implement. Thus, advances in battery technology can serve as a catalyst for the viability of renewable energy, both short and longer term. Alternatively, advances in a hydrogen infrastructure could serve as a storage solution by converting water into hydrogen through renewable sources.

Other infrastructure advancements hold promise for sustainable technologies. Charging stations are a critical infrastructure need to make electric vehicles viable. As mentioned earlier, thousands of public charging stations are available across the United States, and this number is growing. Community development, in general, can be a powerful way that government can influence sustainable opportunities. Advances in transportation, such as the much-hyped hyperloop championed by Elon Musk, are dependent on communities to be tightly clustered to make travel by these means effective.

Investments in roadways more broadly can help unlock the potential of autonomous vehicles, which in turn could help lower automotive consumption and carbon emissions. Research into the benefits of vehicle automation is still in the early stages, but at least one study released in 2016 by researchers at the University of Leeds, the University of Washington, and Oak Ridge National Laboratory estimate that total transportation emissions could be reduced by 40% in a best-case scenario, which includes the availability of other smart transportation technologies to support mass automation on our roadways.[45]

Investments in water-distribution infrastructure, especially in monitoring, could help lead to advancements in technology supporting the efficient use of water and more efficient agricultural practices. Following the lead of energy utilities, water utilities are beginning to use Advanced Metering Infrastructure (AMI) to collect monthly usage data and detect system leaks. Similar to energy meters, smart water meters could also be used to inform customers of real-time consumption and establish a pricing structure that encourages conservation leading up to predicted periods of drought.

In each of these cases, federal and local government can play a critical role in funding needed infrastructure improvements. The 2013 American Infrastructure Report Card, published every four years by the American Society of Civil Engineers to assess the conditions and needs of the country's infrastructure—including energy, roads, waterways, and transit—gave the United States a D+ rating. In fact, this rating has not changed much since 1998 because of delays in maintenance and lack of required investment. The 2013 report claims a gap of $1.6 trillion between what would be needed to maintain current infrastructure and projected funding between 2013 and 2020, or a $200 million shortfall each year.[46]

When government funding for infrastructure is limited, public-private partnerships and multisector partnerships may fill the void. Public-private partnerships are typically contracts where the government outsources infrastructure investment to a private concern, either a for-profit or nonprofit organization. While they have been around for a long time, there clearly has been a trend in increasing use in recent years across the world. There are many examples of successful public-private partnerships. When Union Station in Washington, D.C., fell into disrepair in the late 1970s, the US Department of Transportation and the District, recognizing the enormous cost that would be required to restore the historic building, entered into a partnership with Amtrak and a private developer finding the $160 million needed to move forward. Because of this private-public partnership enough money was raised to not only restore the beauty of the station but also enhance functionality and utility, including the creation of 210,000 square feet of new retail space and a multi-level parking garage.[47]

In countries where a significant percentage of the population lives outside city centers, public-private partnerships are critical to providing that population access to electricity off the grid. In 2011, the DOE, the Treasury, and the Development Bank of Southern Africa came together to create South Africa's Renewable Energy Independent Power Procurement Program (REIPPP). By October 2015, ninety-two projects had been selected through REIPPP, bringing in R193 billion in private investment and 6 MW of renewable capacity.[48] Other examples of public-private partnerships exist around the world in sectors such as transportation, solid waste, and waste-water treatment.

Multisector partnerships are a more recent innovation where government, business, and nonprofits coordinate to create sustained value. In 2006, the NIH launched the Bio-markers Consortium, a partnership with government agencies (e.g., US FDA), private industry (e.g., Pfizer, Merck), and nonprofit organizations (e.g., American Heart Association) that is working to "rapidly identify, develop and qualify potential high-impact biomarkers particularly to enable improvements in drug development, clinical care and regulatory decision-making."[49] Multisector partnerships draw on the expertise and unique perspective of each partner to solve systemic problems.

Alternative Funding of Innovation

Beyond equity from venture capitalists, debt from banks, and grants from government and foundations, a number of alternative investment vehicles have emerged in recent years. First, there has been a proliferation of venture and technology incubators and accelerators worldwide during the past decade. Accelerators are typically short programs, for example, three to six months, designed for nascent ventures that are brought in as a cohort and walked through a curriculum. Ventures admitted to such programs often receive capital, mentoring, and support. For example, Y Combinator offers a standard $120,000 to all admitted ventures to their program, taking a 7% equity stake in the company. Incubators follow a similar model though they do not always admit ventures in cohorts and tend to let ventures stay for longer periods of time (e.g., one to five years). From 2008 to 2014, the number of accelerators in the United States grew an average of 50% each year. There are now estimated to be more than 170 accelerators in existence. Not surprisingly, accelerator programs appear to be concentrated in San Francisco–Silicon Valley, Boston-Cambridge, and New York—these cities account for 40% of all accelerators and two-thirds of funded deals between 2005 and 2015.[50] As of October 2012, there were more than 1,250 incubators in the United States.[51]

As accelerators and incubators have proliferated, so has specialization. There have been a number of prominent examples focused on sustainable technologies. Greentown Labs, the largest green incubator in the United States, is located just outside Boston and houses more than fifty start-up companies in its forty thousand–square–foot facility. With a focus on hardware-based clean technology solutions, the company is sponsored by big companies like General Electric, Shell, and National Grid. Of the 103 companies that have worked through Greentown Labs, 86% are still working on solutions to combat climate change. The Rutgers University EcoComplex in New Jersey has housed several successful sustainable start-ups such as TerraCycle, a recycling company that turns waste into new consumer goods, including hard-to-recycle waste, offering consumers the ability to package and ship waste and earn points toward charity donations. The company, which moved into the EcoComplex in 2004, operates in twenty countries, brings in $20 million annually, and has partnered with Walmart and Home Depot in the United States.[52] Green Spaces houses one hundred firms in New York City and Denver, including Via, an on-demand rideshare company that offers riders affordable transit while reducing carbon emissions. Incubatenergy Network, a consortium of cleantech incubators, brings together EcoComplex, Greentown Labs, and others looking to share resources and collectively support growth of cleantech innovation and development. Started under the National Incubator Initiative for Clean Energy (NIICE), an initiative launched by Energy Secretary Ernest Moniz in 2014, more than 350 companies have been supported by Incubatenergy members, generating more than $330 million in revenue.[53]

Another emerging alternative source of funding is crowdfunding, which has seen exponential growth over the last few years. By 2015, funding raised through crowdfunding surpassed average annual venture capital funding, $34 billion and $30 billion, respectively. The World Bank estimates that global crowdfunding could reach $90 billion by the year 2020.[54] New rules mandated by Title IV of the US Jumpstart our Business Startups (JOBS) Act of 2012 (known as Regulation A+) allow any interested, nonaccredited investors to put up to 10% of their income or net worth into a start-up. Elio Motors, a start-up automaker offering a unique three-wheeled vehicle, benefited greatly from the JOBS Act, raising $102 million through equity crowdfunding from more than six thousand investors and surpassing $1 billion in market valuation after listing its IPO shares in February 2016.[55] Because the vehicle has gas efficiency claims of eighty-four miles per gallon and a sticker price as low as $7,300, the company had more than sixty thousand reservations by the end of 2016.[56] Numerous tech start-ups have emerged to help facilitate the crowdsourcing of equity funding, including gofundme.com and funded.com, which help connect investors with ventures.

Finally, a number of prominent philanthropists have begun to invest directly in the development of clean technologies, and many are starting to join forces to combat climate change. The CREO (Cleantech, Renewables and Environmental Opportunities) Network has brought together more than fifty family offices and foundations who have committed to a collective $300 million investment in sustainable and other social impact initiatives over the next five years.[57] Cleantech Syndicate has grouped more than a dozen wealthy families who have already invested a combined $1.2 billion to clean technologies. With a goal of raising another $1.4 billion over the next five years, Cleantech Syndicate merged with the CREO Network in 2015, renamed the CREO Syndicate, which will represent more than one hundred members with $800 billion in investable capital to put toward sustainable ventures.[58] What makes this different from previous philanthropic efforts is the willingness to provide capital directly to for-profit organizations.

Investor as Visionary Redux

In the end, while some investors with a passion for the environment are willing to sacrifice financial returns to help create sustainable goods and services, by and large investors are going to be motivated by financial returns and risk mitigation. While socially motivated investors can be a powerful force for change, it remains to be seen whether they are sufficient in number to drive the level of disruptive sustainable innovation we believe required. Fortunately, we are seeing experimentation with a number of alternative models from impact investing to crowdfunding that are driving more investment to social aims.

This is not to say that financial returns could not be a significant driver of sustainable investment. The relevant question remains, What is the likelihood of investments in sustainable technologies to create a positive value spread that overcomes the risk of such investment? This again relates to both the demand and supply for sustainable technologies. How expensive will it be to generate, deliver, and scale sustainable technologies, and what is the willingness of consumers to pay for those technologies? These are not easily answered questions. As a result, investment in sustainable technology is fraught with risk characterized by numerous uncertainties that play out over years if not decades.

Ultimately, we know that investment will be required of a diverse set of players. At each phase in the life cycle of a sustainable technology, financial support is needed: from the research lab to an entrepreneurial start-up to a growth company. The capital needed will likely come from a variety of sources—government agencies, venture capitalists, big banks, impact investors, even large incumbent companies. Each will be looking for a return on their investment, be it a financial return or the creation of social value. Collaborations between investors will be necessary—such as public-private and multisector partnerships. The story of Climate Corporation reminds us that entrepreneurs like Friedberg and Khaliq do not succeed on their own. They received support from friends and family, from Khosla Ventures, and eventually from Monsanto. The innovators who seek to usher in a sustainable transformation of business will have no chance without investors willing to take big bets on them.

Chapter 5

CUSTOMER AS KING

LET'S SAY OUR HEROIC MANAGER is able to partner with an innovative genius for a new sustainable technology and is able to secure capital from a visionary investor who shares her enthusiasm for the technology. Good so far, but our innovation journey is not complete. Ultimately, all of us, as consumers, judge whether this new innovation will realize its disruptive potential. According to an old business adage, "The customer is king." Even if businesses produce goods and services with the potential to contribute to sustainability, customers make the most important decision of all, choosing to spend their hard-earned money on something new instead of just sticking with the status quo.

The case of digital programmable thermostats is instructive. These products were first introduced in the 1980s, promising ease of use through push-button programming and "set it and forget it" operation. Because heating and cooling amount to the largest share of energy consumed in the home, programmable thermostats promised significant energy savings. Fast-forward twenty years to 2008. The US EPA suspends its ENERGY STAR programmable thermostat program due to new research suggesting these products were not actually saving more energy than traditional dial thermostats. Why? Consumers were either programming them incorrectly or not bothering to use the programming functions at all. Despite great potential, digital programmable thermostats were plagued by familiar challenges endemic in product development. The product might "work" wonderfully, until it comes into contact with an actual customer.

For digital programmable thermostats to disrupt the market, new products were needed that emphasized creative design, intuitive user interfaces, and smart marketing strategies. While green consumers might exist, there are probably not enough of them to support a true mass-market product. Fortunately, along came Nest Labs. Founders Matt Rogers and Tony Fadell recognized the opportunity to build a smart thermostat that would actually meet consumer expectations. Rogers quit his job at Apple and started Nest Labs out of his garage. First to the market in 2011, the Nest thermostat was designed with a learning algorithm that follows the homeowner's schedule, allowing it to operate independently based on monitoring of consumer behavior, even entering into an energy-save mode if it senses that nobody is at home. They provided one big improvement to the design of the original programmable thermostats; they made it automatic and customized to the consumer.

Their learning thermostat drove new innovation in an otherwise stagnant industry, helping spur the emerging smart home movement. Their insights facilitated a platform on which other products could be built and plugged into, creating a virtuous cycle of sustainable innovations. Five years later, the Nest thermostat is found at mass retailers such as Home Depot, Lowe's, and Best Buy. Seen as a gateway into the home, smart thermostats provided utilities with much-needed data on consumer behavior and access to home systems for demand-side management (DSM) programs. Nest filled two crucial unmet needs that previous products could not: homeowners' need for ease of use and the need to gain access to their own data. Did Rogers and Fadell make the right bet? It appears so. The company sold to Google for $32 billion in 2014.

Nest's success spurred new competitors to enter the smart thermostat market, including incumbents like Honeywell and new start-ups like Ecobee. Market research analysts predict the global market for smart thermostats to reach forty million units ($2.2 billion) by 2022. Once an initial entrant "proves" a market exists for a novel product, other companies soon follow, creating conditions for price competition that make the products more attractive still to new consumers. Google Nest appears well positioned to capture a significant share of this fledgling market.[1] Intuitive design and a deep appreciation for consumer behavior made for a great business, but perhaps more interesting, it created an entire market of tens of millions of consumers who have the data to inform sustainable decision making. Do this thought experiment: Add up the energy savings of an individual consumer forty million times over and you get the value created by data-driven insights. You can then begin to appreciate how sustainable innovations can make an impact at scale.

Every commercially viable innovation from the automobile to aspirin to the smartphone has been ultimately successful because it satisfied a customer need. In fact, it is the potential to fill unmet needs that motivates innovators in the first place. But the innovator or entrepreneur does not always know for certain whether anyone will buy the new gadget or service. History is littered with innovations that never quite caught on with consumers: laser disks in the 1970s; the DeLorian sports car of the 1980s. Apple's Newton, an early personal digital assistant and a precursor to the iPhone, was released in 1993 to much hype and nearly complete disinterest by customers. Some products enjoy brief bouts with success before being overtaken by newer, more desired products. Witness the demise of Blackberry in the face of the iPhone.

One important factor is the "value spread" between the demand for new technology and other existing alternatives. The DeLorian was not attractive given its price and performance relative to other luxury sport cars on the market at the time. As mentioned previously, it is not possible to estimate the demand for renewable energy without taking into account the changing prices for fossil fuels such as natural gas. In 2016, for example, solar energy was cheaper than fossil fuels for the first time.[2]

The basic challenge for sustainable innovations is that these products must create value that exceeds that of alternatives in the marketplace if they hope to have widespread adoption. These innovations can work if enough customers value sustainability and are willing to pay a price premium for sustainable goods. What do we know about consumers' willingness to pay price premiums?

Stated versus Revealed Preferences

A 2015 Nielson Global Survey of Corporate Social Responsibility and Sustainability suggests consumers are indeed willing to pay a price premium for sustainable goods and services—66% of consumers globally say they are willing to pay more for sustainable brands. But challenges still exist, surprisingly, particularly in developed countries.[3] The survey suggests that consumers in *less* developed markets are more willing to invest in these products and services, while those in developed countries such as the United States are harder to influence. Nielson researchers suggest this may be due to the more recent influx of sustainable products and services, including offerings by trusted mainstream brands, and the belief that with so much consumer choice, green should be a basic cost of entry rather than a differentiator. Demand from millennials could be the sea change that sustainability needs to gain traction in the US market. Of millennials surveyed, 73% were willing to pay more for sustainable goods.

But do stated preferences in opinion surveys and marketing panels actually relate to real purchasing decisions? This is a more complicated question. While there are a lot of studies reporting that consumers *say* they will pay more, there are far fewer that show they will actually follow through. For example, in the case of organic foods, the number of people who have favorable opinions about it is significantly larger than those who actually buy it.[4] Researchers have speculated that this disconnect is due to an inherent conflict between "self-interest" and "collective interest."[5] In other words, while it would be in all of our interests to purchase products that conserve the environment, each individual wants to get the best price he or she can. This tension can lead to green products underperforming market expectations.

Sometimes the incessant hype around the benefits to the environment turns customers off. A 2012 *Ad Age* article reported the results from a survey that found that while the vast majority of consumers were taking personal actions to conserve energy, they were becoming slightly less enthused about green products.[6] One reason provided was consumer distrust. They simply could not believe that all of the benefits marketers told them about would actually come from purchasing one more green product. For others, buying green remains a status symbol. Basic psychology dictates that many of us like to show off just how environmentally conscious we are. Thus, we are more likely to put solar panels on the roof where more of our neighbors can see them.[7]

Psychology can be used for more noble ends, however. The field of behavioral economics is full of subtle nudges to get consumers to behave in ways that are aligned with their own long-term interest, whether joining a gym or saving more money. Opower is famous for producing a home energy report that compares your home's energy usage to that of your neighbors. The idea is that this social comparison will encourage you to change your behavior, more so than public service ads or celebrity endorsements. But even here things get complicated. Not all consumers react to these kinds of nudges in the same way. One academic study found that political liberals were much more susceptible to these nudges than conservatives.[8]

Because of social media and greater ease of access to information, there is evidence suggesting that all consumers want greater transparency into a company's actions and may make purchasing decisions based not only on the sustainability of products and services but also on the commitment of the company to be more transparent. For example, while research released by PwC Global in 2016 supports the Natural Marketing Institute findings that customers are most interested in cost (followed by convenience and functionality), 27% of the CEOs surveyed believe that consumers will seek a longer-term relationship with companies that contribute to the greater good of society.[9] It is no longer enough to simply tout sustainable initiatives; brand trust is key to winning consumers.

Clearly, viable green niches exist in numerous industries. Patagonia, Toms of Maine, and Method Cleaners are but a few sustainability-positioned brands. Yet their overall impact remains small. For example, in 2015 the market share of green household cleaning products was estimated to be 3% of the total household cleaner and laundry product market.[10] Research from the Natural Marketing Institute suggests that the well-intentioned US consumer is still highly influenced by price—64% of consumers surveyed expressed an interest in the environment but admitted that they are still price driven when making purchasing decisions.[11] While attitudes can certainly change, sustainability-positioned brands seem to occupy a vibrant but relatively small niche. That does not mean that these companies are not making an impact and do not deserve our praise and respect. Our point is that niche business models will never, on their own, allow business to save the Earth. The mass market needs to change if there is any hope.

Government Intervention

Sometimes, consumer demand for sustainable alternatives does not yet exist. There is a latent demand waiting to be unearthed. In these instances, governments can help stimulate demand for sustainable technologies through government procurement. Over the last seven years, the US government has spent more than $1 trillion a year on goods and services.[12] With this kind of spending, the government can certainly drive the direction of innovation by asking for specific requirements from vendors. One example is the requirement that all new federal buildings must be LEED certified. This step helped drive wide adoption of the LEED standard across the United States, even outside the government sector.

Another example is that all federal agencies are required by law to purchase products that are either ENERGY STAR–certified or meet performance requirements set forth by the DOE's Federal Energy Management Program (FEMP).[13] FEMP provides US agencies with the training and guidance needed to meet their energy management goals. In some sectors, such as information technology, where government is a large and highly influential customer, this regulation has resulted in new, energy-efficient technologies being offered both to US agencies and the private market. However, despite its influence, the government is only one consumer. Despite the hundreds of billions spent by the US government, it still represents only 14.3% of GDP.[14] Government purchasing may help create markets, but it is unlikely to sustain them.

As an alternative to using its purchasing power, the government can manipulate prices directly. Through interventions in the market, government can bypass reluctant consumers and play a direct role in shaping the attractiveness of sustainable innovation. Government has a number of policy levers to provide direct financial incentives to aid the commercialization of innovative sustainable products and services, helping stimulate demand. Such interventions are certainly not without controversy. They tend to create what economists refer to as "deadweight losses," where higher prices suppress demand, leading to a loss of value for both consumers and producers. Moreover, we should also be cautious about whether government intervention is authentically targeted at increasing the public good or toward propping up politically connected individuals and industries. The important but vexing question is whether the societal benefit created by such interventions makes up for the deadweight loss and potential for abuse.

The most obvious price manipulations are tax incentives and subsidies for new technologies. In the United States, subsidies for solar energy attract the most attention. Investment tax incentives were first introduced to the marketplace through the Energy Policy Act of 2005, offering a 30% credit for residential and commercial systems placed into service during between January 1, 2006, and December 31, 2007. This tax credit has been extended several times, including a multi-year extension included in the 2015 Omnibus Appropriations Act that would credit projects completed by the end of 2023. According to the Solar Energy Industry Association (SEIA), the incentive facilitated the installation of 27 gigawatts (GW) of US solar energy by the end of 2015 (cumulative) and will reach nearly 100 GW by the end of 2020. In the second quarter of 2016, solar energy accounted for 64% of all new electricity-generating capacity brought online, more than coal, natural gas, and nuclear combined. Further research shared by SEIA show that the cost to install solar panels has dropped by more than 70% over the last ten years.[15]

While such tax incentives and subsidies are effective, one challenge is that they effectively choose winners and losers in the battle for a dominant technology. Even within the broad scope of clean technology, there is uncertainty about which technologies have the most promising future. What if the subsidy is encouraging investment in a technology that with further investment we learn is not promising or, even worse, does not deliver the hoped-for environmental benefits? It is not always easy, politically, to end subsidies once they start. Witness the subsidies for corn-based ethanol in the United States. Pushed by congressional representatives from corn-growing states, the federal subsidies for corn-based ethanol has been bashed by many as picking the (wrong) technology. Some estimates suggest that corn-based ethanol is just as carbon intensive as gasoline when change in land use is included in the calculation.[16] But when subsidies begin, powerful constituencies can develop around them, collecting support from influential legislators and sustaining themselves in the face of mixed or weak evidence of public benefits.

Tax incentives and subsidies are not the only levers available to government. On the other side of the spectrum, there are so-called sin taxes for dirty technologies. Taxes on cigarettes, up to 45% of the overall cost of a carton,[17] have arguably helped suppress demand. The number of adult smokers in the United States dropped from 40% in 1965 to below 20% in 2012.[18] Perhaps even more telling is the drop in adolescent smoking from 27% in 1991 to 11% in 2015.[19] Higher taxes coupled with new regulations about tobacco use in public places and warnings on packaging, as well as public campaigns against smoking by government and other interest groups, has led to innovation in "smokeless" alternatives such as vapor. In this manner, sin taxes can also drive the direction of innovation as firms strive to create new products with more favorable margins.

Consider gasoline taxes in the United States and Europe, which have had an impact on driving habits of car owners. Automobile usage tends to be rather inelastic in the short run; in other words, people are locked into their cars and commuting patterns and do not change their consumption much as prices vary. However, in the mid- to long run people can adjust their behavior to lower gasoline consumption. For example, they can purchase fuel-efficient vehicles, adjust where they live and work to lower commute distances, and seek out public transportation. However, the effect of taxes may very well be swamped by the general changes in gasoline prices driven by global oil markets. In the United States, the average state gasoline tax has risen by 20% over the past ten years,[20] while average gasoline prices have fallen nearly 40% from their peak in 2012.[21] The federal tax on gasoline has stayed flat since the early 1990s at 18.4 cents.

Germany adopted an alternative approach, using what are called feed-in tariffs (FITs) to incentivize the adoption of renewable energy, in particular, solar PV cells. Different energy sources are charged differentially, effectively taxing those whose energy comes from fossil-fuel sources. In Germany, these FITs also came with twenty years of fixed compensation for electricity produced by these solar cells. The creation of such incentives encouraged the production of solar cells and arguably inspired innovation to both improve performance and lower costs. Today, Germany hosts more than one-third of solar capacity globally and successfully disrupted the wholesale electricity market. Renewable generation grew from zero to 20% of energy production between 1990 and 2012.[22]

Regulatory Manipulations

There are other ways that government can intervene beyond price manipulations that can have an impact on demand and hence incentivize sustainable innovation. In the electric utility industry, the renewable portfolio standard (RPS) has been effective in creating demand for solar and wind installations by utilities. An RPS requires electric utilities to have a certain percentage of their electricity generated by renewable sources by a specific date. In the United States, twenty-nine states (plus Washington, D.C., and two US territories) have RPS. The most aggressive RPS, in Maine, requires that 40% of electricity generated in the state must come from renewable sources such as solar and wind by 2017.[23]

An RPS is effectively a regulation that requires certain behaviors or prohibits others, monitors whether an organization complies with those requirements, and can levy sanctions against an entity for failing to do so. In the United States, the Corporate Average Fuel Economy (CAFE) standard for automobiles is another prominent example. First adopted in 1975, CAFE standards require that the fleet of cars sold by a given producer in the United States must have an average fuel efficiency specified by the regulation. From 1990 to 2010, the

CAFE standard stayed at 27.5 miles per gallon (mpg) for passenger vehicles before more recently being raised to 35.5 mpg by 2016 and 54.5 mpg by 2025.[24] In the fine print, the new CAFE standards provide automakers with a sliding scale based on their "footprint," which is determined by wheelbase and track in square feet. Thus, each manufacturer will have a different CAFE requirement that is averaged across its fleet. The new CAFE standards will cut GHG emissions in half by 2025, or six billion metric tons over the life of the program, which is more than total 2010 US emissions.[25] According to the US DOT Bureau of Transportation Statistics, despite the flat CAFE standards (pre-2011), the average for passenger vehicles had risen to 30 mpg by 2005,[26] suggesting that in addition to regulation there were other market influences at play.

New CAFE standards will push the industry further, and the industry seems to be meeting targets ahead of schedule. The "Draft Technical Assessment Report" released by the EPA and National Highway Traffic Safety Administration (NHTSA) in July 2016, as part of a midterm evaluation of the industry's ability to meet the new 2022–2025 standards, found that a wider number of cost-effective technologies exists than originally evaluated in 2012 when setting the standards and that automakers are already overcomplying with existing standards. What is also interesting is that despite the new interest in hybrid and electric vehicles, new gasoline technologies will drive the compliance.[27] Would automakers be inclined to invest in those new technologies without regulation? Perhaps, but arguably not at the rate that they are doing so today.

Creating Demand via Standards and Labeling

There are political and practical constraints to government intervention. As a result, there are numerous private efforts under way to help consumers spend their money on sustainable products. Information disclosure is one popular approach. The logic is that consumers would make more sustainable choices if they had the appropriate information at the right time. While government may provide that role, for example, mandating restaurants to display their sanitation ratings, it is often private or nonprofit organizations that step up into this role. For example, developers did not have a standard for what constituted a green building and certainly no way to reliably communicate that to customers until the US Green Business Council helped define it through the LEED certification. Such standards and certification solve what economists call information asymmetries, in which one party to a transaction has better information than another. By creating a standard, and coupling it with a robust certification program that validates industry claims, consumers can have confidence that their purchase is in fact green.

Sustainability standards and labels have been crafted in numerous industries (see Figure 5 for a few of the most prominent examples). In the United States, the most successful example is arguably the market for organic foods. Before the US Department of Agriculture (USDA) established an organic foods label, consumers were inundated with competing claims of the environmental friendliness of various food products. Only after the USDA established a standard, simple label in 2002 for organic foods were people assured of company claims, contributing to the steady increase in demand for organic foods. Between 2004 and 2014, sales of organic foods had grown from $14 billion to $35 billion.[28] Organic foods have become ubiquitous in the United States, sold through specialty local grocers and high-end chains such as Whole Foods as well as low-price discounters such as Walmart and Target. In 2015, organic food sales represented almost 5%

FIGURE 5   Prominent environmental standards and labels.

of the market, and organic food growth rate (10.8%) far surpassed that of the overall food market (3.3%).[29] Note that a simplistic "regulation is bad for business" mantra would have predicted the opposite pattern. But information-based regulations can help drive demand by providing much-needed credibility in nascent markets.

Other standards and labeling have proved successful, particularly in empowering consumers to make sustainable choices. In 2001, the Marine Stewardship Council (MSC) first introduced its certified sustainable seafood label into the marketplace in collaboration with international food and consumer goods company Unilever. Unilever sold a number of fish products and wanted to ensure the sustainability of its supply chain. The company partnered with the World Wildlife Fund, a nonprofit looking for ways to stop overfishing and the collapse of fisheries around the world. Both parties agreed that a global market-driven approach would be the best path forward to reward fisheries with good management practices and encourage change in others. Via a globally recognized label, they would help create consumer demand for sustainably sourced fish. MSC was created as a third-party nonprofit to ensure credibility and consumer trust in the program. To be MSC certified, fisheries must meet the MSC Fisheries Standard, first developed by scientists, fishing industry stakeholders, and conservation groups in 1998 and recently updated in 2014. Fisheries are evaluated against twenty-eight performance indicators focused on maintaining adequate fish stocks, minimizing environmental impact, and effectively managing operations for long-term sustainability and productivity. By 2015, MSC-certified fisheries represented close to 10% of the total global wild-caught seafood supply, with major retailers and brands across the world making commitments to 100% sourcing of MSC-certified products, including McDonald's.[30]

Another example is the FSC, created in the 1990s by businesses and environmentalists frustrated with the lack of global agreement to stop deforestation. Similar to the MSC, the FSC takes a market-driven approach toward forest protection, using product-certification standards and a highly recognized label to identify products that are sustainably sourced. This ensures not only that the wood has come from a sustainably managed forest but also that it is isolated and not mixed in with noncertified wood as it makes its way through the supply chain and onto retail shelves. By 2016, more than thirty-five million acres were FSC certified, and the label is gaining traction at retailers, including IKEA, who committed to 100% sourcing of wood, paper, and cardboard products that are either FSC certified or recycled by 2020.[31]

In all these examples, we see the creation of market demand by solving an information asymmetry that allows consumers to purchase sustainability-oriented products. In each case, a collection of individuals and organizations collaborated to create, enforce, promote, and educate consumers about the standard. In the case of organic foods, the government played a direct role in helping solve information asymmetries between producers and consumers. By establishing and enforcing a standard, the government can help expose latent demand for sustainable products and thus create downstream incentives for innovators to pursue sustainable technologies.

However, in the case of the MSC sustainable seafood label, a major multinational corporation, Unilever, played a critical role. Enterprise involves a web of interactions with suppliers, retailers, distributors, and alliance partners. These business partners may create demand for sustainable innovation. Sometimes downstream buyers can motivate change up the supply chain. Unilever was motivated to solve the information asymmetry around sustainable fisheries as a way to create premium products. To be clear, it was not running the fisheries. It purchased fish from fisheries. Yet the company felt pressures from its customers to address sustainable fishing. As a result, Unilever took a lead in creating incentives up the supply chain to sustainably fish and partnered with an otherwise unlikely partner in the World Wildlife Fund, who shared the same vision, albeit each had different internal drivers.

These supply-chain initiatives can be powerful drivers of change. Interestingly, they all derive from the incentives for those downstream companies to require environmental compliance. What motivates downstream companies to push sustainability? For Home Depot, carrying FSC-certified wood is in response to consumer demand for sustainable timber. Walmart is trying to provide sustainability-friendly products to consumers while minimizing its own costs. In this way, Walmart is passing the costs of creating sustainability up the supply chain. What we see in these examples is that the power of customers need not be limited to individuals making decisions online or in a retail store. Government is a key customer that can drive change as well. And powerful customers in the supply chain that link businesses can wield tremendous power, as demonstrated by Walmart's impact on sustainability.

The Influence of Activists and Nongovernmental Organizations

There is also an important role for NGOs and activists to influence consumers by creating awareness about the environmental impact of certain products. These actions can actually be incredibly supportive of innovation in some cases. At first glance, NGOs and innovators seem to be at opposite ends of the spectrum. Activists are often seen as prohibiting—looking to stop pollution or environmentally impactful activity. Innovators are about creating—looking for new ways to deliver value and to meet market needs. But in many ways, they are two sides of the same coin. Innovators may be responding to market opportunities created by activist actions and the social movements they create.

In perhaps the most famous example of this dichotomy, consider the case of DuPont and CFCs. As public pressure increased from NGOs to phase out CFCs to reduce the size of the hole in the ozone layer, DuPont—the largest manufacturer of CFCs—first argued against the need to restrict them, all the while investing in research and development in alternative technologies. Once DuPont realized it had a viable alternative, HFCs, it changed its stance and lobbied for the Montreal Protocol, which banned CFCs. By innovating a solution, DuPont was able to convert what was a low-margin commodity business (CFCs) into a higher-margin business in which it had a significant intellectual property (i.e., patent) position (HFCs).[32]

Of course, activists are not the only players in the arena trying to influence consumers and the rules of the game. Companies with opposing views on environmental regulation are
easily matching and collectively exceeding spending by activists. According to the Center for Responsive Politics, Exxon-
Mobil spent almost $12 million in lobbying alone in 2015.[33]
Collectively the oil and gas industry spent nearly $130 mil-
lion in 2015.[34] The result has been an arms race in lobbying
dollars with heightened in-fighting and paralysis in Congress.
The reality is that environmental lobbyists cannot compete
with deep company pockets. However, spending data published by the center suggest that activist efforts and rising public concern about the environment could be impacting private industry lobbying dollars—in 2007, reported spending
was $86 million but averaged $145 million between 2008 and
2015,[35] with presumably much of this spending allocated to either climate change efforts directly or preservation of the status quo.

Interestingly, despite stiff resistance from some parts of the
private sector, climate initiatives were gaining ground on Cap-
itol Hill in the early 2000s. During the Bush administration,
a new level of acceptance on climate change action emerged
with the passing of the 2005 Energy Policy Act and 2007 Energy Independence and Security Act, despite opposing lobbying efforts. Some environmentalists argue that significant savings were left on the table for the sake of passing the bills, but
it was progress nonetheless. Conversely, under the Obama administration there was no significant environmental legislation passed. Interestingly, this aligns with the sharp increase
of spending by the oil and gas lobbyists starting in 2008. Frustrated with the lack of action of Congress, President Obama
resorted to executive actions—like the 2015 Clean Power Plan.

Given the difficulty in passing new legislation, activists began increasingly to pursue what emeritus Stanford professor David Baron refers to as "private politics," leveraging the courts and/or the court of public opinion to directly force companies to adopt sustainable policies and practices. Through civil lawsuits, activists have sought to create a direct financial consequence to firms who pollute or despoil the environment. Through high-visibility campaigns such as protests and boycotts, activists seek to draw attention to issues and shame companies into taking action to avoid damaging their brands and hurting demand for their products and services.

Businesses are often responsive to these threats as a risk-mitigation strategy to prevent or limit damage to their brands. In our own research, we find evidence that if targeted, larger and more visible businesses are more likely to comply with stakeholder pressures.[36] Their size and visibility make them more susceptible to activist pressure. Even proxy votes, of which the overwhelming number fail to gain support from a majority of shareholders, can be effective, as business leaders will on occasion respond to them to avoid bad publicity. Similarly, rarely do boycotts reach such widespread adoption that they have a significant impact on demand, but once again companies frequently try to address, or at the very least manage, the concerns to avoid broader brand damage. In all of these cases, concerns about bad press and its broader impact on consumer demand and the impact on important stakeholders in the business have a more substantial impact on behavior than the narrow harm caused by the activist action.

Thus, activists often look for the most visible way to make their case. In April 1995, protesters from Greenpeace chained themselves to the Brent Spar deepwater drilling rig to be decommissioned by Royal Dutch Shell and forced the company to dismantle the structure on land instead of dumping it in the ocean. Twenty years later, instead of using chains, activists are using a more effective, less dangerous means to bring visibility to offending companies and arguably having better success—social media. Greenpeace put pressure on fashion brand Burberry via a three-day social media blitz using familiar outlets like Twitter, Facebook, and Instagram in tandem with in-person protests across six countries to force the company to commit to removing toxic, perfluorinated chemicals from its manufacturing process by 2020.

Interestingly, the threat of a large group of well-resourced activists with global support may not be as big as a threat as an artful viral video by a couple of amateurs. In 2016, the social activist Sofia Ashraf created a "parody rap video" against consumer goods maker Unilever in India, accusing it of dumping mercury in Kodaikanal. The video went viral, gaining more than three million viewers. Overnight, Unilever had a public relations disaster to deal with. The ubiquity of social media has allowed for more and more people to have a voice in public debates. This increases pressure on companies who have little way of knowing when, by whom, and how they may be scrutinized.

It is important to recognize that not all businesses are susceptible to such tactics. In our own research, we have found that firms that have well-recognized brand names are more susceptible to activist campaigns, likely because they have much to lose in brand identity and customer loyalty. However, upstream producers of goods and services not directly consumed by the average customer may be inoculated from such activist actions. Thus, activists will often target downstream retailers rather than the producers themselves. For example, activists went after furniture retailer IKEA for not using sustainable wood rather than the forestry industry itself. Greenpeace and other activists have launched a national campaign against genetically modified seafood, targeting some big names in the grocery sector. Despite a 2015 FDA approval of AquaBounty's genetically modified salmon, the product is meeting significant market resistance due to commitments by heavyweights like Safeway, Kroger, Target, Trader Joe's, Aldi, and Whole Foods not to carry the fish.[37]

It is equally important to recognize that not all activist groups are as effective in their private campaigns. In our own work, we have found that more aggressive tactics are, not surprisingly, more effective. Interestingly, however, we have found that controlling for the tactics used, the most effective activist actions are those undertaken by groups not clearly identified as environmental activists. In general, the public and consumers assume that Greenpeace and the Sierra Club will take aggressive stances against firms. As a result, their actions may be dismissed by some as the raging of outlier activists.

So how does activist pressure translate into more sustainable products on the market? By raising the costs of poor environmental behavior, they create incentives for firms to innovate new products and services that ameliorate environmental concerns. In addition to selling assets to finance a $20 billion compensation fund for victims,[38] BP reportedly invested $500 million into an effort to revamp the brand following the Deepwater Horizon disaster.[39] Rather than have to continue to deal with periodic outbursts and poor publicity, it is far better for businesses to innovate to avoid impacts in the first place, as did former General Motors CEO Rick Wagoner, who argued for GM's investment in electric vehicles and hydrogen fuel cells as a way to remove automobiles from the climate debates.[40]

In some cases, activists will work directly with companies to try to innovate solutions. In the United States, the Environmental Defense Fund (EDF) has arguably been the most aggressive in doing so. Started as a legal fund for environmental actions, the EDF began experimenting with collaborations with companies in the early 1990s. One of the earliest successes was a collaboration with McDonald's to replace its Styrofoam containers with recycled paper. Today, the EDF, through its Climate Corps program, partners with companies such as Apple, Google, and General Motors to place graduate students in summer internships to help identify solutions to environmental challenges faced by the organizations. Many of the Climate Corps fellows go on to hold long-term sustainability positions at these organizations.

Activists and NGOs are important players in the broader institutional environment in which businesses operate. They can be adversaries, and they can be partners with businesses. They can be catalysts for broader sociopolitical change that provides incentives to companies to innovate new sustainable products and services. They are also constrained. They require resources, often financial. They are often in competition with one another for donations and attention. Social media has given voice to literally thousands of new activists. They can vary greatly in their approach and tactics. While not every business is susceptible to their various tactics, they can impact consumer perceptions and ultimately the demand for certain products and services.

Customer as King Redux

The customer is indeed king. Business cannot save the Earth without consumers choosing sustainable goods and services from available alternatives. But only a small number of consumers will go out of their way to buy sustainable products, particularly at a price premium. Sometimes consumer demand is hindered by poor information and market imperfections. In these instances, government can intervene to manipulate prices and demand that sustainable technologies are made more attractive to buyers, but this can be politically unattractive. Empowering consumers with information about the environmental impact of various products and services may help expose latent demand that motivates the innovation of sustainable technologies, but only if such latent demand exists. Activists and other NGOs can help further spur demand by raising awareness and shifting preferences among customers, but they are often challenged with balancing the urgency of the message with something that will resonate with the general public.

What should give us hope is that customer preferences are shaped by culture and incentives and sometimes do shift. What can drive these changes? Stakeholders, including the media and activists, can surely play a role. Activists and NGOs may work to raise awareness on the issue. Scientists and journalists may bring further attention to a specific sustainability issue or bad actor. Government may eventually weigh in, providing guidance, incentives, or regulation to try to move markets. Downstream buyers may see a market opportunity and work with upstream suppliers to ameliorate concerns. Finally, an enterprising entrepreneur may see an opportunity to redefine the market and launch a new product or service that addresses the burgeoning demand in an innovative way.

Under the right conditions, norms can shift quickly. For example, bisphenol A (BPA) is an industrial chemical used in a variety of products, including plastic water bottles. When concerns were raised about possible health effects of BPA on the brain, behavior, and prostate gland of fetuses, infants, and children, the reaction was swift.[41] Parents immediately started seeking alternatives, and a cottage industry in BPA-free water bottles quickly arose. The innovation engine kicked in, providing new alternatives to meet the shift in demand.

Anecdotally, norms seem to shift quickest whenever there is a direct threat to one's health or that of one's children. Many environmental challenges, however, have diffuse impacts in the distant future. Climate change is particularly vexing, as scientists talk about impacts on fifty-year time lines or "at the end of the century." An entire academic discipline in marketing and consumer behavior attempts to understand shifts in markets. A related discipline in sociology tries to understand the emergence of social movements that sometimes give birth to new industries. What is clear is that it is hard to predict when social norms will shift and demand will evolve.

Perhaps the most impactful shift that could help with our sustainability challenges would be if lower consumption became the norm. One way that may occur is through the emergence of radical new business models that redefine markets. Uber and Airbnb are pioneering a set of new business models in what is referred to as the sharing economy. Latent demand was unlocked by radical takes on established markets by upstart entrepreneurs. They were enabled by technology, specifically the ubiquity of smartphones, but ultimately represented new business models. Similarly, Matt Rogers and Tony Fadell innovated a new product, the Nest thermostat, but the real impact is how it enables information to unlock latent demand for energy-efficient heating and cooling in the home. Their success was not preordained but emerged from the interaction of a number of actors who influenced the sociopolitical-economic system that in turn helped spur demand.

Chapter 6

SYSTEM AS CATALYST

CAN BUSINESS SAVE THE EARTH? The answer depends on a broad system of forces: forces that generate new inventions, that successfully commercialize new products out of these inventions, that provide capital to support commercialization and scaling, and that provide value to a wide number of customers. Each of these forces is driven by the idiosyncratic ingenuity and persistence of daring and creative individuals and depends on a robust institutional setting to create the conditions for these individuals to thrive. Meeting our sustainability challenge will require massive innovation across multiple industrial sectors. The only way to have any hope for such a dramatic change is with a systemic solution that catalyzes these forces. What might that solution look like?

Let's return to the example of Tesla. Founded in 2003 by Martin Eberhard and Marc Tarpenning, a $7.5 million series A round of financing brought in Elon Musk as an investor and chairman of the board. Subsequent rounds of venture investment raised capital from the likes of the VC firm Draper Fisher Jurvetson, Google founders Larry Page and Sergey

Brin, JP Morgan Chase's venture investment fund, and German automaker Daimler AG. Despite great promise and this influx of capital, Tesla struggled early on, as many nascent ventures do.

Musk was named CEO in October 2008, when he promptly laid off a quarter of Tesla's workforce. In June 2009, with the future of the US auto industry and broader economy appearing bleak, Tesla took a $465 million loan from the US DOE through the Advanced Technology Vehicle Manufacturing Program. Prospects began to brighten. By 2010, Tesla was posting profits on the strength of its second-generation Roadster. A partnership with Toyota was announced, and designs for the forthcoming Model S were released. A date was set for its IPO to be underwritten by Goldman Sachs and other investment banks. At the end of June 2010, Tesla went public on the Nasdaq stock exchange and raised $226.1 million.

Government financial incentives via the 2008 Energy Improvement and Extension Act and the 2009 American Recovery and Reinstatement Act had helped drive consumer interest and demand in electric cars as well as the building out of a vast fueling support network: more than fourteen thousand charging stations and close to thirty-seven thousand charging outlets in the United States, according to the DOE. And while the increases in US fuel-efficiency standards were intended to be technology neutral, electric car technologies were the best positioned to capitalize on the inevitable industrywide shift toward a more fuel-efficient economy.

Complementary activism by organizations like Plug in America have also helped pave the way for electric vehicles. This nonprofit group has worked to raise awareness of the benefits of electric vehicles and encourage adoption of the technology through engaging policy makers on incentives, such as the federal tax incentive and high-occupancy vehicle (HOV) status for electric vehicles in states such as California. The organization has also joined forces with other electric vehicle supporters, Sierra Club and Electric Auto Association, to host National Drive Electric Week to showcase technologies and educate consumers at coordinated events across the United States. In addition to finding support among green organizations combating climate change, electric vehicles have also been bolstered by groups advocating US energy independence.

By the summer of 2013, Tesla had paid back its loan from the federal government, and the company's stock price had increased from less than $20 per share to more than $50. By early 2014, the stock price had risen sharply to more than $200 per share. With the introduction of the more affordable Model 3 and movement into battery manufacturing, investors continue to bet on the company, with the price hovering above this $200 mark, hitting a high of $280 in July 2015. By April 2017, Tesla was the most valuable car company in America.[1]

Is Elon Musk a visionary? Yes, definitely. We need such businesspeople to see a future that none of us can yet grasp. But Musk had support from scientists and engineers who made small discoveries that, when aggregated, led to massive leaps forward. He managed his company effectively, forging alliances with other large organizations. He had investors willing to place long-term bets and even the help of the federal government's patient capital. Along the way he received critical support from providers of complementary assets, government support for buyers, and activists. All of these factors made his task of winning over customers a bit easier and lifted the electric car from the pages of science fiction into garages all across America.

∽

If business is to save the Earth, we will need many Elon Musks to be sure. But we will need more of everything else in this story too. The genius innovator who envisions a better future. The heroic business leader who turns these dreams into reality. The smart investor who can see the next big trend before it unfolds. The passionate activist and the engaged government official who shape the rules of the game. The consumer who passes the final judgment whether an innovation is viable. Each is a cog in the innovation wheel and plays an important role in meeting our sustainability challenge.

But each also faces binding constraints. Great inventions do not become products unless there is a business case and an organization in which to house a compelling business model. Even long-term investors need to make a return. Customers may say they love the environment, but they also seek to buy goods and services at a reasonable price. No matter where someone sits in the system, it pays to be aware of the constraints of the other players and be creative about ways to alleviate them. That is the only way for our innovation system to reach its full potential.

One of the key pillars of this book is that innovation does not occur in a vacuum. New goods and services emerge out of the interplay of numerous actors and countless actions. The journey to disruptive sustainable technologies is likely a sinuous one. A promising technology may begin in a university professor's laboratory funded by a grant from the federal government. That technology may be licensed to an entrepreneur who launches a new venture around that technology. The entrepreneur may then seek funding from a venture capitalist to further test and refine the technology. Eventually the entrepreneur launches the product and learns whether customers are willing to pay for it. As the business scales, additional funding may be needed to build production facilities or supply chains. Perhaps a grant from a federal agency or a loan from a bank is sought. Or maybe the entrepreneur takes the company public and raises capital on a public exchange. Or the company is acquired by a larger business who has the resources to support scaling.

All along the way, the technology is competing with alternatives—both existing products and services and new technologies vying to be the disruptor. Actions big and small can determine whether the technology achieves its disruptive potential. It could be a new product-labeling scheme that creates the conditions under which customers can finally recognize the value provided by the new innovation. Or it could be an environmental activist group that embraces the new technology and puts pressure on government to adopt policies more favorable to that technology. There could also be a large incumbent player, heavily invested in an older legacy technology, which actively lobbies government to stall or kill the new kid on the block. Or an unexpected technological leap in a completely different domain might render this heretofore promising idea simply unworkable or undesirable. The path to success is not easy to predict.

Unlocking the Power of the Innovation System

What can we do to invigorate the innovation system and ensure the best chance to search for and commercialize disruptive sustainable technologies? We need the concerted effort of numerous stakeholders: innovators, managers, investors, consumers, federal policy makers, state and local officials, activists, the media, foundations, NGOs, universities, and individual citizens. We will need to harness the power of each of these players to have the best chance to save the Earth. Here are some thoughts on what each can do.

Innovators

For those intrepid innovators among our readers, our advice is simple: go do it! At its most basic level, innovation is a numbers game. Most new technologies and businesses are going to fail. That is the nature of innovation and entrepreneurship. The more people who experiment, the more likely that a disruptive sustainable technology will emerge. Even those who fail help push the innovation system forward—discovering potential paths forward and identifying paths that are unlikely to succeed and thus should be avoided. Of course, from both an individual and society perspective, we would like more success than failure, but that is where others can help.

Managers

Most big companies today are worried about disruption. This suggests that more resources will be poured into being the cutting edge of technology rather than to preserving old worlds. This is a good thing for our sustainability challenge. For large companies, this involves partnering with universities and research labs and investing in, and in some cases purchasing, entrepreneurial ventures. Rather than use so much precious capital to lobby for regulations protecting the old industry, why not use more of it to invest in sustainability-oriented funds or issue green bonds? Challenge employees to do more in their personal and professional lives to support sustainability. Ask suppliers to pursue sustainable products and services. Finally, invest in the complementary products and resources that will allow disruptive innovations to flourish. Your firm many not invent the disruptive technology, but you can still capture value from it by possessing crucial complementary assets, such as manufacturing and distribution capability.

Investors

Private investors are the fuel for the innovation engine. Allocating capital to the best ideas is the most important task. Sustainable innovations vary greatly in both their risk profile and potential payback time. Diversity in funding mechanisms is critical. Some ventures will lend themselves to traditional venture capital. Others will require more patient capital. Thus, we encourage investors to innovate novel funding mechanisms that address this diversity of needs. Crowdfunding, impact investing, green bonds, and equity-based incubators are all relatively new and intriguing vehicles for advancing sustainable technologies. We should keep experimenting with alternative funding models.

Consumers

We suggest that consumers consume less, but when making purchases, buy more sustainable goods. Of course, this is not as simple as it sounds. How does one know if a given product or service is sustainable? To find out, demand transparency. Require producers to explain the environmental impact of their goods. This may require some coordination, lobbying for the government or third parties to create labeling programs or certification schemes. But if you can make it work, you can change the marketplace such that what works for the environment wins. That could be the single greatest contribution any individual could make toward our sustainability challenge.

Federal policy makers

Government is the enemy of innovation, right? Not necessarily. Smart federal policy can be an incredible catalyst for innovation. Basic R&D is a public good that is not easily financed in the private sector. Federal funding of research toward sustainable technologies is critical. Extended patent protection for sustainable technologies and creation of innovation prizes are two other ways to turbocharge innovation efforts. Policy can also encourage more competition and entrepreneurial entry. For example, reduce regulatory and paperwork burdens for entrepreneurs getting started and create rules that encourage crowdfunding and other creative ways to finance start-ups. In addition, push for strong antitrust enforcement that prevents concentration of market power that may thwart innovation. On the consumer side, federal policy makers can put a price on carbon. We know this seems politically impossible today. This reality does not absolve them from responsibility. In the meantime, federal policy makers can consider other levers. For example, they can create more product labels and certifications that help consumers make informed decisions and use the vast purchasing power of government to drive the diffusion of these certifications. Finally, the federal government can make a major push for infrastructure investment, such as a smart electrical grid, that could bring about entrepreneurial efforts in clean technologies.

State and local officials

Federal policy is not the only government-oriented catalyst for innovation. State and local officials also can play a vital role, particularly since we know that innovation clusters in certain geographic areas. States can pass B Corp legislation that encourages business to formally incorporate sustainability goals into their charters. States can leverage their purchasing power to buy green and invest pensions and other investment dollars in socially responsible funds. Perhaps most important, they can help build robust entrepreneurial ecosystems in their cities and regions. For example, economic development officials can strive to build innovation districts focused on sustainable technologies. School administrators can endeavor to incorporate STEM and entrepreneurship training in primary and secondary schools.

Activists and the media

Activists and the media can play a critical role in the broader innovation ecosystem. They can help drive customer sentiments toward green goods and services by raising awareness of the environmental challenges we face. This information can help drive transparency in both products and investments. They can simultaneously punish laggards and celebrate innovative leaders. These actions can be critical, as emergent technologies are often stigmatized at first precisely because they are new and a threat to the existing order. All of this will take discipline from activists and the media. Fear of the unknown and the risks of unintended consequences make many activists wary of innovation. But innovation is the only way we can meet our sustainability challenge. We encourage activists to consider partnering with innovators to find creative solutions to our sustainability challenges. Resisting change is not an option.

Foundations and NGOs

Foundations and NGOs have a number of ways to push for disruptive sustainable innovations. They can fund innovators and entrepreneurs pushing the envelope on sustainable technologies. Impact investing is a powerful concept that holds much promise for sustainable technologies, especially when these ideas have long payback periods and high uncertainty around them. Foundations and NGOs can help energize investors more broadly by partnering with capital providers to help create transparency and accountability in sustainable investing. These entities can also directly impact researchers and innovators through the creation of innovation prizes and by funding research grants. Finally, they can help catalyze the overall innovation system by supporting education efforts in STEM and related disciplines in primary and secondary schools and higher education.

Universities

Universities provide fuel to the innovation engine. They can push for more research into disruptive sustainable technologies. Equally important, they can help facilitate the progression of technologies from the lab to the marketplace. They can help commercialize sustainable technologies by tapping into and supporting the entrepreneurial spirit of their faculty, students, and alumni. Finally, similar to foundations, they can help catalyze the overall innovation system by doubling down on the emphasis on technical fields and the education of STEM students.

Individual citizens

Each and every one of us can serve as a catalyst in our roles as concerned citizens. We can become an inventor ourselves or work for an innovative venture dedicated to sustainable technologies. We can be an impact investor, investing our savings in socially responsible funds or becoming an angel investor in cleantech ventures either directly or through a crowdfunding site. We can be conscientious consumers, buying sustainable goods and services and demanding transparency from those we purchase from. We can be innovators, perhaps volunteering at a local incubator or mentoring an entrepreneurial venture. And finally, we can be involved in the broader system, lobbying government and elected officials to push for policies that produce sustainable innovation.

A New Moon Shot

In 1961, President John Kennedy inspired a generation with his audacious pledge to put a person on the moon by the end of the decade. Climate change and our broader sustainability challenges require a new moon shot—one as audacious as, if not more so than, the race to the moon. We need to generate action to innovate across numerous sectors, such as energy, transportation, agriculture, and the built environment. We need sustainable innovations that will disrupt these markets and significantly reduce the environmental impact of these sectors.

To accomplish this, we will need more "shapers"—individuals and groups who work to cause the innovation system to deliver sustainable technologies.[2] Elon Musk of Tesla is more than just a businessperson; he has shaped the entire innovation system in a positive direction. So have Vinod Khosla of Khosla Ventures and Fred Krupp of the Environmental Defense Fund. Each is an example of a shaper. And there are so are many others—in universities, large corporations, and the federal government. Each plays a distinct but critical role in advancing disruptive sustainable innovations. And we need all of them and more to save the Earth.

Ultimately, there are no silver bullets. Driving both the rate and direction of innovative activity is hard. There is not a single recommendation that alone is sufficient to accomplish the task. There are simply no easy solutions to the environmental challenges we face, and there are no easy prescriptions to generate the scale of disruptive innovation we argue is needed. It will take action, many actions, by many individuals, each playing perhaps a small role but that together can bring about significant change. That is what system change looks like.

In the face of such complexity, one may be tempted to lose faith, to believe that the efforts of any one individual are insufficient and, worse yet, inconsequential. We reject this logic. We are optimistic about the capacity of individuals to push the innovation system forward. We need to recognize that our sustainability challenge is not just an environmental issue but an economic issue, a social issue, a question of our national competitiveness, and a question of our general well-being. The evolution of markets and technology will play itself out over decades. Actions to influence this trajectory may take years to have a meaningful impact. Thus, we need to consider the levers—all the levers—that can help lead the system to generate more disruptive sustainable technologies and pull those levers when opportune or politically possible.

In a speech on the Apollo space program to a crowd at Rice University in 1962, President Kennedy famously said, "We choose to go to the Moon and do these things . . . *not* because they are easy, but because they are hard; because that goal will serve to organize and measure the best of our energies and skills, because that challenge is one that we are willing to accept, one we are unwilling to postpone, and one we intend to win." We are optimists by our nature. A sustainability moon shot will be hard, but we believe in the innovative potential of markets and the potential for all of us to work together to catalyze the innovation system to meet our sustainability challenges.

Business as Savior Redux

Can business save the Earth? The stakes could not be higher. John Sterman, a systems dynamics professor at MIT, likes to

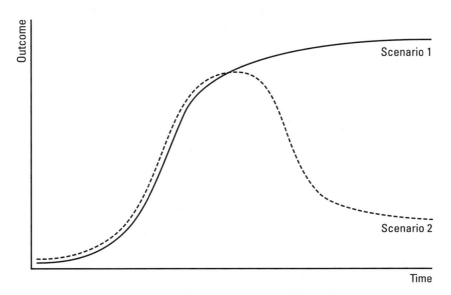

FIGURE 6   Possible outcomes of a natural dynamic process.

illustrate what is at risk in the following way. A simple graph
of world population growth over time shows, not surprisingly,
exponential growth. He argues that no natural system persists with exponential growth forever. There has to be a level-
ing off at some point (see Figure 6). In the best of worlds, population growth follows a simple sigmoid curve and levels off at
some sustainable level—scenario 1. More likely are overshoot,
decline, and possible collapse—scenario 2. In other words, we
will see a significant decrease in world population as natural
ecosystems become stressed and population exceeds the capacity for Earth to support.

Not addressing our sustainability challenges, and in particular climate change, will mean rising sea levels, altered weather
patterns, and migration of agriculture away from once vibrant
areas. Humans can adjust, but what will such an adjustment
look like? Mass displacement of the most at-risk populations?
Starvation on a massive scale? Horrendous wars as people fight
over natural resources such as water and arable land? Collapse

of nation-states? These scenarios are not just some fantastic vision of a dystopian future. These very scenarios may already be playing themselves out on a regional scale. Some observers believe the desertification driven in part by climate change in the Middle East has led to conflicts over water and agricultural land that have manifested themselves in the uprisings, wars, and terrorist activity that have long plagued the region.[3] It does not take too much imagination to wonder how these forces could lead to an unraveling in other places in the world. Imagine fifty million Bangladeshis displaced because of rising sea levels. Envision a United States where the American South is disproportionately affected by climate change, exacerbating regional inequalities and tensions.

How can we avoid these potentially devastating outcomes? Business has to be part of the solution. In particular, we need to catalyze markets to create disruptive sustainable technologies that will displace existing technologies across a wide number of sectors. We need innovative new products, services, and business models that will create value for consumers in new ways while substantially reducing environmental impacts. Such transformation will not merely be driven by a few heroic entrepreneurs or innovative geniuses. Nor will it be driven solely by the actions of government or nonprofit organizations or even the wealthiest investor or the most sophisticated consumer. It will take all of those players and more to work as a system, driving rapid innovation across multiple sectors simultaneously. We all have the power, in one way or another, to serve as a catalyst. The question before us, all of us, is whether we will take the actions today to create the conditions under which the innovation system can thrive. The fate of our planet depends on it.

NOTES

Chapter 1

1. "Advertising Spend: Worldwide," Digital Strategy Consulting, July 22, 2009, www.digitalstrategyconsulting.com/intelligence/2009/07/advertising_spend_worldwide.php.

2. Tracey S. Keys and Thomas W. Malnight, "Corporate Clout Distributed 2012: The Influence of the World's Largest 100 Economic Entities," Global Trends, 2010, 2, www.globaltrends.com/product/special-report-corporate-clout-distributed-2012-the-influence-of-the-worlds-largest-100-economic-entities/.

3. Ibid., 13.

4. Ibid., 5.

5. World Commission on Environment and Development, *Our Common Future: The Brundtland Report* (New York: Oxford University Press, 1987), 1.

6. "U.S. and World Population Clock," US Census Bureau, accessed September 20, 2016, www.census.gov/popclock/world.

7. Bruce Pengra, "One Planet, How Many People? A Review of Earth's Carrying Capacity," UNEP Global Environmental Alert Service (GEAS), June 2012, 3, https://na.unep.net/geas/archive/pdfs/GEAS_Jun_12_Carrying_Capacity.pdf.

8. R. K. Pachauri, L. A. Meyer, and Core Writing Team, IPCC, eds., *Climate Change 2014: Synthesis Report. Contribution of Working Groups I, II and III to the Fifth Assessment Report of the Intergovernmental Panel on Climate Change* (Geneva, Switzerland: IPCC, 2014), Topic 1(1.1), 40.

9. Ibid., Topic 1(1.2), 44.

10. Ibid., Topic 2(2.2), 58.

11. "Understanding the IPCC Reports," World Resources Institute, accessed September 2016, http://www.wri.org/ipcc-infographics.

12. Marshall Burke, Solomon M. Hsiang, and Edward Miguel, "Global Non-linear Effect of Temperature on Economic Production," *Nature* 527,

no. 15725 (November 12, 2015): 235–239, http://www.nature.com/nature
/journal/v527/n7577/full/nature15725.html.

13. Pachauri, Meyer, and IPCC, *Climate Change 2014: Synthesis*, 73.

14. "Water Scarcity," UN Water, accessed September 2016, http://www
.unwater.org/water-facts/scarcity/.

15. US Department of Defense, *National Security Implications of Climate-Related Risks and a Changing Climate*, US DOD, July 23, 2015, RefID:
8-6475571.

16. "Manage the Nitrogen Cycle," NAE Grand Challenges for Engineering, accessed May 2017, http://www.engineeringchallenges.org
/challenges/nitrogen.aspx.

17. "Species Extension—the Facts," IUCN Red List, May 2007,
cmsdata.iucn.org/downloads/species_extinction_05_2007.pdf.

18. Lauretta Burke, Kathleen Reytar, Mark Spalding, and Allison
Perry, "Reefs at Risk Revisited," World Resources Institute, February 2011,
www.wri.org/publication/reefs-risk-revisited.

19. "The State of the Air 2016," American Lung Association, 2016,
www.lung.org/our-initiatives/healthy-air/sota/key-findings.

20. "Where Nutrient Pollution Occurs," Nutrient Pollution, US Environmental Protection Agency, accessed September 2016, www.epa.gov
/nutrientpollution/where-nutrient-pollution-occurs.

21. "Nutrient Pollution—Finding Solutions," Ohio Environmental Protection Agency, accessed September 2016, epa.ohio.gov/dsw/wqs
/NutrientReduction.aspx#146064464-background.

22. "Nitrogen & Phosphorus," Chesapeake Bay Foundation, accessed
September 2016, www.cbf.org/how-we-save-the-bay/issues/agriculture
/nitrogen-phosphorus.

23. Janet L. Sawin, Kristin Seyboth, and Freyr Sverrisson, *Renewables
2016 Global Status Report* (Paris: REN21 Secretariat, 2016), 6. REN21 is an
international nonprofit and network of energy policy stakeholders with a
goal of advancing renewable technologies worldwide.

24. Greentech Media, "Venture Capital Investment in Green Technologies Back to Pre-recession Levels with $1.9B in Q3 2009," September 30,
2009, www.greentechmedia.com/images/wysiwyg/PR/Q309VC.pdf.

25. US Energy Information Administration, *Levelized Cost and Levelized Avoided Cost of New Generation Resources in the Annual Energy Outlook
2015*, Table 1: Estimated Levelized Cost of Electricity (LCOE) for New
Generation Resources 2020, June 2015, https://www.eia.gov/outlooks
/archive/aeo15/pdf/electricity_generation_2015.pdf.

26. Jeremy Quittner, "Top 10 Venture Capital–Backed Green Compa-

nies," *Inc. Magazine*, April 21, 2015, www.inc.com/jeremy-quittner/venture
-capital-flows-to-sustainability-companies-and-earth-day.html.

27. John F. Ehrenfeld, *Flourishing, A Frank Conversation about Sustainability* (Stanford, CA: Stanford University Press, 2013).

28. Jeremy Hall, Greg Daneke, and Michael Lenox, "Sustainable Development and Entrepreneurship: Past Contributions and Future Directions," *Journal of Business Venturing* 25, no. 5 (2010): 439–448.

29. Steven Levitt and Dubner Stephen, *Superfreakonomics: Global Cooling, Patriotic Prostitutes, and Why Suicide Bombers Should Buy Life Insurance* (New York: William Morrow, 2009), 8–12.

30. Microsoft, "Environmental Sustainability," 2017, https://www
.microsoft.com/en-us/about/corporate-responsibility/environmental
-sustainability.

31. "This Is UPS: Committed to More," UPS, accessed October 2017,
https://sustainability.ups.com/.

32. Governance & Accountability Institute Inc., "Flash Report: 81% of
S&P 500 Companies Published Sustainability Reports in 2015," March 15,
2016, www.ga-institute.com/nc/issue-master-system/news-details/article
/flash-report-eighty-one-percent-81-of-the-sp-500-index-companies
-published-corporate-sustainabi.html.

33. WWF, Ceres, Calvert Investments, and David Gardiner and Associates, "Power Forward 2.0: How American Companies Are Setting Clean
Energy Targets and Capturing Greater Business Value," WWF, June 19,
2014, 2, https://www.worldwildlife.org/publications/power-forward-2-0
-how-american-companies-are-setting-clean-energy-targets-and-captur
ing-greater-business-value.

34. 3M, "2016 Sustainability Report," 13, accessed September 2016,
http://multimedia.3m.com/mws/media/1214315O/2016-3m-sustainabil
ity-report.pdf.

35. Michael Lenox, Andrew King, and John Ehrenfeld, "An Assessment of Design-for-Environment Practices in Leading U.S. Electronics
Firms," *Interfaces* 30, no. 3 (2000): 83–94.

36. Vikas Vij, "Green Product Sales Up Average 91% for GE, Dow,
Others," *GreenBiz*, July 20, 2015, https://www.greenbiz.com/article/green
-product-sales-average-91-ge-dow-others.

37. Philips, "Philips Increases Sales of Green Products to 54% of Total Sales," press release, February 23, 2016, www.philips.com/a-w/about
/news/archive/standard/news/press/2016/20160223-Philips-increases
-sales-of-Green-Products-to-54-per-cent-of-total-sales.html.

38. Andrew King and Michael Lenox, "Lean and Green? Exploring

the Spillovers from Lean Production to Environmental Performance," *Production and Operations Management* 10, no. 3 (2001): 244–256.

39. Joseph A. Schumpeter, *Capitalism, Socialism, and Democracy* (New York: Harper Brothers, 1942), 84.

40. "Nuclear Power in France," World Nuclear Association, updated August 2017, www.world-nuclear.org/information-library/country-profiles /countries-a-f/france.aspx.

41. Ibid.

Chapter 2

1. Li Zhou, "Creating Plastics from Greenhouse Gases," *Smithsonian. com*, May 1, 2015, www.smithsonianmag.com/innovation/creating-plastic -from-greenhouse-gases-180954540.

2. Ibid.

3. Wendy Kock, "Plastic Made from Pollution Hits U.S. Market," *USA Today*, December 30, 2013, www.usatoday.com/story/news/nation/2013 /12/30/plastic-from-carbon-emissions/4192945/.

4. Cara Santa Maria, "Newlight Technologies: Pollution to Plastic," video by KCET TV, SoCal Connected, accessed August 27, 20017, https:// www.kcet.org/shows/socal-connected/newlight-technologies-pollution -to-plastic-0.

5. Newlight Technologies, "Newlight Raises $9.2 Million in Series C Financing Round to Expand AirCarbon Commercialization: Newlight to Expand the Commercial-Scale Production of AirCarbon Using Patented Greenhouse Gas-to-Plastic Technology," press release, April 2, 2014, https://www.newlight.com/newlight-raises-9-2-million-in-series-c -financing-round-to-expand-aircarbon-commercialization-newlight-to -expand-the-commercial-scale-production-of-aircarbon-using-patented -greenhouse-gas-to-plastic/.

6. Newlight Technologies, "Newlight Signs 10 Billion Pound Production License with IKEA," press release, March 1, 2016, newlight.com /newlight-signs-10-billion-pound-production-license-with-ikea-2/.

7. Malcom Gladwell, "Hallelujah," *Revisionist History*, Season 1, Episode 7, 2016, www.revisionisthistory.com.

8. Darrell Etherington, "Over $1B in Gorilla Glass Sales in 2012 Helps Propel Corning to New Single Quarter Sales Record," *Tech Crunch*, January 29, 2013, techcrunch.com/2013/01/29/over-1b-in-gorilla-glass-sales -in-2012-helps-propel-corning-to-new-single-quarter-sales-record/.

9. Gijs P. A. Mom and David A. Kirsch, "Technologies in Tension: Horses, Electric Trucks, and the Motorization of American Cities, 1900–

1925," *Technology and Culture* 42, no. 3 (2001): 489–518, doi:10.1353/tech.2001.0128.

10. Philip Anderson and Michael L. Tushman, "Technological Discontinuities and Dominant Designs: A Cyclical Model of Technological Change," *Administrative Science Quarterly* 35, no. 4 (1990): 604–633, www.jstor.org/stable/2393511.

11. Nancy W Stauffer, "Solar Photovoltaic Technologies: Silicon and Beyond," MIT Energy Initiative, December 14, 2015, http://energy.mit.edu/news/solar-photovoltaic-technologies.

12. Richard Martin, "First Solar's Cells Break Efficiency Record," *MIT Technology Review*, March 3, 2016, https://www.technologyreview.com/s/600922/first-solars-cells-break-efficiency-record/.

13. Benjamin F. Jones, "The Burden of Knowledge and the 'Death of the Renaissance Man': Is Innovation Getting Harder?," *Review of Economic Studies* 76, no. 1 (2009): 283–317; Stefan Wuchty, Benjamin F. Jones, and Brian Uzzi, "The Increasing Dominance of Teams in Production of Knowledge," *Science* 316, no. 5827 (2007): 1036–1039.

14. Henry Chesbrough, "Open Innovation: The New Imperative for Creating and Profiting from Technology" (Boston: Harvard Business School Press, 2003).

15. Wesley M. Cohen and Daniel A. Levinthal, "Absorptive Capacity: A New Perspective on Learning and Innovation," in "Technology, Organizations, and Innovation," special issue, *Administrative Science Quarterly* 35, no. 1 (1990): 128–152.

16. Richard Pérez-Peña, "Patenting Their Discoveries Does Not Pay Off for Most Universities, a Study Says," *New York Times*, November 20, 2013, http://www.nytimes.com/2013/11/21/education/patenting-their-discoveries-does-not-pay-off-for-most-universities-a-study-says.html.

17. Gary Dushnitsky and Michael J. Lenox, "When Does Corporate Venture Capital Investment Create Firm Value?," *Journal of Business Venturing* 21 (2006): 753–752.

18. Unfortunately, IPXI was unable to overcome the patent industry's reluctance to get deals done without litigation, which IPXI was trying to avoid, and the organization closed its doors just five years later.

19. "Clean Energy Patent Growth Index 2014 Year in Review," Clean Energy Patent Growth Index, Cleantech Group–Heslin Rothenberg Farley & Mesiti P.C., April 17, 2015, http://www.cepgi.com/2015/04/2014-year-end.html#more.

20. W. M. Cohen, R. R. Nelson, and J. P. Walsh, "Protecting Their Intellectual Assets: Appropriability Conditions and Why U.S. Manufactur-

ing Firms Patent (or Not)," working paper no. W7552, National Bureau of Economic Research, 2000.

21. US Patent and Trademark Office, "2701: Patent Term [R-07.2015]," in *Manual of Patent Examining Procedure*, 9th ed., chap. 2700, sec. 2701, revised November 2015, https://www.uspto.gov/web/offices/pac/mpep /s2701.html.

22. Ansari XPRIZE, October 4, 2004, http://ansari.xprize.org/.

23. "Past Prizes" and "Active Prizes," XPRIZE, accessed October 2016, http://www.xprize.org/past-prizes.

24. "Fuel Cell Technologies Office Accomplishments and Progress," US DOE Fuel Cell Technologies Office, April 2016, https://energy.gov/eere /fuelcells/fuel-cell-technologies-office-accomplishments-and-progress.

25. "Sustainable Living: The Unilever Sustainable Living Plan," Unilever, accessed October 2016, www.unilever.com/sustainable-living/the -sustainable-living-plan.

26. Rahul Kapoor and Nathan R. Furr, "Complementarities and Competition: Unpacking the Drivers of Entrants' Technology Choices in the Solar Photovoltaic Industry," *Strategic Management Journal* 36 (2015): 416–436, doi:10.1002/smj.2223.

27. "Clean Energy Patent Growth Index 2014 Year in Review."

28. "California Green Innovation Index: International Edition," Next 10, May 18, 2015, http://next10.org/international. Note that "investment" includes venture capital, debt/loans, grants from public and private sources, private and public equity, and follow-on public offerings.

29. Ibid.

30. "2016 California Green Innovation Index," Next 10, June 29, 2016, http://next10.org/2016-gii.

31. Steve Bowers, vice president, marketing and communications of APEX, e-mail communications with Michael Lenox, January 2017.

32. Michael Lenox, Dan Bierenbaum, Mary Margaret Frank, and Rachna Maheshwari, "Winning the Green Innovation Economy: An Analysis of Worldwide Patenting," UVA Darden School of Business, Batten Institute for Entrepreneurship and Innovation, April 2012, http:// www.darden.virginia.edu/uploadedFiles/Darden_Web/Content/Faculty _Research/Research_Centers_and_Initiatives/Batten_Institute/Re search/Publications/BB_WinningGreenEconomy.pdf.

33. Ken Auletta, "Analysis of Higher Education: Get Rich U.," *New Yorker Magazine*, April 30, 2012, www.newyorker.com/magazine/2012/04/30 /get-rich-u.

34. "US Colleges and Universities—Utility Patent Grants, Calendar Years 1969–2012," US Patent and Trademark Office, Patent Technology Monitoring Team, accessed October 2016, https://www.uspto.gov/web /offices/ac/ido/oeip/taf/univ/univ_toc.htm.

35. "US Patent Statistics Chart Calendar Years 1963–2015," US Patent and Trademark Office, Patent Technology Monitoring Team, accessed October 2016, www.uspto.gov/web/offices/ac/ido/oeip/taf/us_stat.htm.

36. Jamie Beckett, "Study Shows Stanford Alumni Create Nearly $3 Trillion in Economic Impact Each Year," *Stanford News*, October 24, 2012, news.stanford.edu/news/2012/october/innovation-economic-impact -102412.html.

37. Edward B. Roberts, Fiona Murray, and J. Daniel Kim, "Entrepreneurship and Innovation at MIT Continuing Global Growth and Impact," MIT Sloan School of Management, December 2015, http://web.mit.edu /innovate/entrepreneurship2015.pdf.

38. Beckett, "Study Shows."

39. Roberts, Murray, and Kim, "Entrepreneurship and Innovation at MIT."

40. Michael Lenox, Andrew King, Charles Easley, and Asif Mehedi, "The Economic Impact of Entrepreneurial Alumni: A Case Study of the University of Virginia," UVA Darden School of Business, Batten Institute for Entrepreneurship and Innovation, December 2014, https://web3 .darden.virginia.edu/uva-alumni/.

Chapter 3

1. "Electric Vehicle Charging Station Locations," US DOE Alternative Fuels Data Center, accessed October 2016, www.afdc.energy.gov /fuels/electricity_locations.html.

2. Tesla Motors Energy Press Kit, 2017, www.tesla.com/presskit /teslaenergy.

3. "Tesla Makes Offer to Acquire SolarCity," *Tesla Motors* (blog), June 21, 2016, www.tesla.com/blog/tesla-makes-offer-to-acquire-solarcity.

4. Aaron K. Chatterji and Michael W. Toffel, "The Power of C.E.O. Activism," *New York Times*, April 1, 2016, https://www.nytimes.com/2016/04 /03/opinion/sunday/the-power-of-ceo-activism.html.

5. Michael W. Toffel, Aaron K. Chatterji, and Julia Kelley, "CEO Activism (A)," Harvard Business School, Case Study N9-617-001, March 2017 (revised October 2017), http://www.hbs.edu/faculty/Pages/item.aspx ?num=52500.

6. Google, accessed October 2017, https://www.google.com/intl/en /about/our-company/; Microsoft, accessed October 2017, https://www .microsoft.com/en-us/about.

7. "2012–2013 SUSB Employment Change Data Tables," US Census Bureau, updated October 3, 2016, www.census.gov/data/tables/2013 /econ/susb/2013-susb-employment.html.

8. Laura Holson, "An Environmentalist's Latest Laundry List," *New York Times*, February 23, 2011, www.nytimes.com/2011/02/24/fashion /24HOLLENDER.html?_r=0.

9. Dual-class stock is defined by Investopedia as "stocks such as Class A and Class B shares, where the different classes have distinct voting rights and dividend payments. Two share classes are typically issued: one share class is offered to the general public, and the other is offered to company founders, executives and family. The class offered to the general public has limited voting rights, while the class available to founders and executives has more voting power and often provides a majority control of the company." Dual-class stocks allow founders and other executives to retain majority voting power even without a significant equity in the company. Investopedia, accessed October 2017, http://www.investopedia.com /terms/d/dualclassstock.asp.

10. Jillian D'Onfro and Eugene Kim, "Google's Co-founders Are about to Sell $4.4 Billion Worth of Shares," *Business Insider*, February 13, 2015, www.businessinsider.com/googles-co-founders-are-going-to-sell-44 -billion-worth-of-shares-2015-2.

11. Preferred stock is defined by Investopedia as "a class of ownership in a corporation that has a higher claim on its assets and earnings than common stock. Preferred shares generally have a dividend that must be paid out before dividends to common shareholders, and the shares usually do not carry voting rights." Investopedia, "Preferred Stock," accessed October 2017, http://www.investopedia.com/terms/p/preferredstock.asp ?ad=dirN&qo=investopediaSiteSearch&qsrc=0&o=40186.

12. Antony Page and Robert A. Katz, "The Truth about Ben and Jerry's," *Stanford Social Innovation Review*, Fall 2012, ssir.org/articles/entry /the_truth_about_ben_and_jerrys.

13. "Tom's of Maine Sells Out to Animal Testing Giant Colgate-Palmolive: Another One Bites the Dust," *Animal Rights Information and News Resource* (blog), March 23, 2006, geari.blogspot.com/2006/03/toms-of -maine-sells-out-to-animal.html; Louise Story, "Can Burt's Bees Turn Clorox Green?," *Business Day*, January 6, 2008, www.nytimes.com/2008/01/06 /business/06bees.html; Jumana Farouky, "Anita Roddick, the Queen

of Green," *Time*, September 11, 2007, content.time.com/time/business/article/0,8599,1660911,00.html.

14. B Lab, 2017, www.bcorporation.net.

15. Caroline Preston, "The 20 Most Generous Companies of the Fortune 500," *Fortune*, June 22, 2016, fortune.com/2016/06/22/fortune-500-most-charitable-companies/.

16. In general, estimates for the total number of companies worldwide are difficult to source. See "Listed Domestic Companies, Total," The World Bank (data sourced from the World Federation of Exchanges database), accessed August 28, 2017, data.worldbank.org/indicator/CM.MKT.LDOM.NO?end=2015&start=1975&view=chart.

17. Henry Taylor, "Who Is the World's Biggest Employer? The Answer Might Not Be What You Expect," *World Economic Forum*, June 17, 2015, www.weforum.org/agenda/2015/06/worlds-10-biggest-employers/.

18. Steve Schaefer, "The World's Largest Companies 2016," *Forbes*, May 25, 2016, www.forbes.com/sites/steveschaefer/2016/05/25/the-worlds-largest-companies-2016/#4247f21a37eb.

19. "GDP (Current US$)," The World Bank, accessed November 2016, data.worldbank.org/indicator/NY.GDP.MKTP.CD.

20. Derek Wong, "UN Estimates Annual Global Environmental Costs Equal $6 Trillion," *Environmental Leader*, October 5, 2010, www.environmentalleader.com/2010/10/05/un-estimates-annual-global-environmental-costs-equal-6-trillion/.

21. Adi Ignatius and Daniel McGinn, "Novo Nordisk CEO Lars Sørensen on What Propelled Him to the Top," *Harvard Business Review*, November 2015, hbr.org/2015/11/novo-nordisk-ceo-on-what-propelled-him-to-the-top.

22. "Bill George on Rethinking Capitalism," interview by McKinsey & Company, December 2013, www.mckinsey.com/global-themes/leadership/bill-george-on-rethinking-capitalism.

23. Matteo Tonello, with James Reda of Arthur J. Gallagher & Co., "CEO and Executive Compensation Practices: 2015 Edition," The Conference Board, September 15, 2015, corpgov.law.harvard.edu/2015/09/15/ceo-and-executive-compensation-practices-2015-edition/.

24. Theo Francis and Joann S. Lublin, "CEOs Awarded More Cash Pay," *Wall Street Journal*, April 21, 2015, www.wsj.com/articles/ceos-awarded-more-cash-pay-1429608602.

25. Dominic Barton and Mark Wiseman, "Focusing Capital on the Long Term," McKinsey & Company, December 2013, www.mckinsey.com/global-themes/leadership/focusing-capital-on-the-long-term.

26. Steve Dennis, "Why Tim Cook Doesn't Care about the 'Bloody ROI,'"

Forbes, March 7, 2014, www.forbes.com/sites/stevedenning/2014/03/07 /why-tim-cook-doesnt-care-about-the-bloody-roi/#d285ae640b3e.

27. Andrew Whitten, "Why Are There So Few Public Companies in the U.S.?," The National Bureau of Economic Research, October 14, 2016, http://www.nber.org/digest/sep15/w21181.html.

28. Grace Wong, "Green Groups Strut Their Stuff on Wall Street," CNN Money, February 26, 2007, http://money.cnn.com/2007/02/26 /news/economy/txu_green/index.htm?postversion=2007022617.

29. Unfortunately, one thing the new owners could not control was the fall of natural gas prices in the years preceding the buyout, forcing Energy Holdings Group to file for bankruptcy. The investors, based on historical data, made a bet that electricity consumption would continue to rise and so would prices. Shortly after the buyout, natural gas prices started declining and the company could not compete with electricity being supplied by natural gas power plants. Losing money and unable to make a dent in the $48 billion paid taking the company private, Energy Holdings Group filed for bankruptcy protection under Title 11 in 2014.

30. Julie Appleby, "Many Who Lost Savings, Jobs Pleased," *USA Today*, May 26, 2006, usatoday30.usatoday.com/money/industries/energy/2006 -05-25-enron-workers-usat_x.htm.

31. Economic Policy Institute, "Top CEOs Were Paid 276 Times More Than the Typical Worker in 2015," press release, July 12, 2016, www.epi .org/press/top-ceos-were-paid-276-times-more-than-the-typical-worker -in-2015/.

32. Jeff Klein, "The Four Principles of Conscious Capitalism," *Conscious Connection Magazine*, May 19, 2014, www.consciousconnectionmagazine .com/2014/05/four-principles-conscious-capitalism/.

33. Daniel Esty and Andrew Winston, *Green to Gold: How Smart Companies Use Environmental Strategy to Innovate, Create Value, and Build Competitive Advantage* (New York: Wiley, 2009).

34. Andrew King and Michael Lenox, "The Locus of Profitable Pollution Reduction," *Management Science* 48, no. 2 (2002): 289–299.

35. Shameek Konar and Mark A. Cohen, "Does the Market Value Environmental Performance?," *Review of Economics and Statistics* 83, no. 2 (2001): 281–289.

36. Technically, we would also want to factor in both the cost of the sustainability initiative and the opportunity cost of the next best alternative investment to calculate the net present value of the sustainability investment opportunity.

37. Andrew King and Michael Lenox, "Lean and Green? Exploring the Spillovers from Lean Production to Environmental Performance," *Production and Operations Management* 10, no. 3 (2001): 244–256.

38. "The Business Case for Zero Waste," General Motors, accessed October 2017, https://www.gm.com/content/dam/gm/en_us/english /Group3/sustainability/sustainabilitypdf/GMs_Landfill-free_Blueprint .pdf.

39. Andrew King, "Retrieving and Transferring Embodied Data: Implications for the Management of Interdependence within Organizations," *Management Science* 45, no. 7 (1999): 918–935.

40. Cone Communications, "New Cone Communications Research Confirms Millennials as America's Most Ardent CSR Supporters," press release, September 23, 2015, www.conecomm.com/news-blog/new-cone -communications-research-confirms-millennials-as-americas-most -ardent-csr-supporters.

41. Henry Sauermann and Wesley M. Cohen, "What Makes Them Tick: Employee Motives and Firm Innovation," *Journal of Management Science* 56, no. 12 (2010): 2134–2153.

42. Ibid.

43. "100 Best Companies to Work For," *Fortune Magazine*, 2012, archive .fortune.com/magazines/fortune/best-companies/2012/snapshots/73 .html; Ron Ruggless, "Hospitality Turnover Rose to 72.1% in 2015," *Restaurant News*, March 23, 2016, nrn.com/blog/hospitality-turnover-rose -721-rate-2015.

44. Gail Sullivan, "Starbucks to Help Baristas with Bill for Online College," *Washington Post*, June 16, 2014, www.washingtonpost.com/news /morning-mix/wp/2014/06/16/starbucks-to-help-baristas-with-bill-for -online-college/.

45. Tim Greiner, "Sustainable Supply Chains: Can Retailers Be the Rising Tide That Lifts All Boats?," Sustainable Brands, July 2, 2015, www .sustainablebrands.com/news_and_views/supply_chain/tim_greiner /sustainable_supply_chains_can_retailers_be_rising_tide_lifts.

46. "Walmart Sustainability Index Program," Walmart, accessed October 2017, https://www.walmartsustainabilityhub.com/sustainability -index.

47. Ibid.

48. Christopher Matthews, "10 Ways Walmart Changed the World," *Time*, July 2, 2015, http://business.time.com/2012/07/02/ten-ways-wal mart-changed-the-world.

49. "Sustainability Leaders: Sustainability Index," Walmart, accessed June 29, 2015, http://corporate.walmart.com/global-responsibility/environment-sustainability/sustainability-index-leaders-shop.

50. "Wood Purchasing Policy," Home Depot, accessed October 2017, https://corporate.homedepot.com/sites/default/files/image_gallery/PDFs/Wood_Purchasing_Policy_2017.pdf; "Sustainable Forestry," Home Depot, accessed October 2017, http://ecooptions.homedepot.com/sustainable-forestry/

51. "Kalundborg: Case Study," International Institute for Sustainable Development, accessed July 2, 2015, https://www.iisd.org/business/viewcasestudy.aspx?id=77.

52. Sam Goss, Gareth Kane, and Graham Street, "The Eco-Park: Green Nirvana or White Elephant?," Clean Environment Management Centre, University of Teesside, United Kingdom, 2006, https://www.tees.ac.uk/docs/DocRepo/Clemance/Ecopark.pdf.

53. Accenture and the United Nations Global Compact, "The UN Global Compact—Accenture CEO Study on Sustainability 2013," September 2013, https://www.unglobalcompact.org/docs/news_events/8.1/UNGC_Accenture_CEO_Study_2013.pdf.

54. Jeffrey G. York and S. Venkataraman, "The Entrepreneur-Environment Nexus: Uncertainty, Innovation, and Allocation," *Journal of Business Venturing* 25 (2010): 449–463.

55. Joseph A. Schumpeter, *Capitalism, Socialism and Democracy* (New York: Routledge, 2013), 83–84, https://books.google.com/books?hl=en&lr=&id=MRg5crpAOBIC&oi=fnd&pg=PR2&dq=capitalism+socialism+and+democracy+schumpeter&ots=oIYvWj8krY&sig=OffEI2LdtXm6NJXVT30_hxTqVN4.

56. Aron S. Spencer and Bruce A. Kirchhoff, "Schumpeter and New Technology Based Firms: Towards a Framework for How NTBFs Cause Creative Destruction," *International Entrepreneurship and Management Journal* 2, no. 2 (2006): 145–156.

57. Kai Hockerts and Rolf Wüstenhagen, "Greening Goliaths versus Emerging Davids—Theorizing about the Role of Incumbents and New Entrants in Sustainable Entrepreneurship," *Journal of Business Venturing* 25, no. 5 (2010): 481–492.

58. Tom Randall, "Here's How Electric Cars Will Cause the Next Oil Crisis," *Bloomberg*, February 25, 2016, https://www.bloomberg.com/features/2016-ev-oil-crisis/.

Chapter 4

1. Food and Agriculture Organization of the United Nations, "2016: The State of Food and Agriculture, Climate Change, Agriculture, and Food Security," Executive Summary, 2016, xi, http://www.fao.org/3/a -i6030e.pdf.

2. "The Climate Corporation," Khosla Ventures, accessed November 2016, http://www.khoslaventures.com/portfolio/climate-corporation; Bruce Upbin, "Monsanto Buys Climate Corp for $930 Million," *Forbes*, October 2, 2013, www.forbes.com/sites/bruceupbin/2013/10/02/monsanto -buys-climate-corp-for-930-million/#6e3557265ae1.

3. "MoneyTree Report Data: Thomas Reuters," Pricewaterhouse-Coopers/National Venture Capital Association, Investments by Industry Q1 1995—Q2 2016 (Excel Tables, Total US by Quarter and Year tab) (online site discontinued).

4. Ibid. (Excel Tables, Clean Tech and Ranking tabs) (online site discontinued).

5. Ibid. (Clean Tech tab) (online site discontinued).

6. "Venture Capital and Cleantech: The Wrong Model for Clean Energy Innovation," MIT Energy Initiative Working Paper, July 2016, https:// energy.mit.edu/wp-content/uploads/2016/07/MITEI-WP-2016-06.pdf.

7. Aaron Chatterji, Rodolphe Durand, David Levine, and Samuel Touboul, "Do Ratings of Firms Converge? Implications for Strategy Research," *Strategic Management Journal* (forthcoming); Aaron Chatterji, David Levine, and Michael Toffel, "How Well Do Social Ratings Actually Measure Corporate Social Responsibility?," *Journal of Economics and Management Strategy* 18, no. 1 (2009): 125–169.

8. Aaron Chatterji and Michael Toffel, "How Firms Respond to Being Rated," *Strategic Management Journal* 31 (2010): 917–945; Olga Hawn, Aaron Chatterji, and Will Mitchell, "How Financial Market Legitimacy Conditions Change in Social Legitimacy: The Impact of Additions and Deletions by the Dow Jones Sustainability Index," April 23, 2013, https:// faculty.fuqua.duke.edu/~ronnie/bio/DJSI-2013-04-23.pdf.

9. The Forum for Sustainable and Responsible Investment, "Report On US Sustainable, Responsible and Impact Investing Trends," 2016, http://www.ussif.org/trends.

10. "Stanford to Divest from Coal Companies," *Stanford News*, May 6, 2014, https://news.stanford.edu/news/2014/may/divest-coal-trustees-050 714.html; Larry Gordon, "UC Sells Off $200 Million in Coal and Oil

Sands Investments," *LA Times*, September 9, 2015, http://www.latimes
.com/local/education/la-me-ln-uc-coal-20150909-story.html.

11. "Vision Statements," Dominican Sisters of Caldwell, 2015, cald
wellop.org/about-us/mission-vision/.

12. "Corporate Stance on Climate Change," Dominican Sisters of
Caldwell, 2015, caldwellop.org/where-we-stand/corporate-stances/.

13. "The Ceres Roadmap for Sustainability," Ceres, accessed December 2016, www.ceres.org/roadmap. The Ceres Principles were replaced
in 2010 by the Ceres Roadmap for Sustainability, which provides a more
detailed look at the risks and opportunities in shifting to a more sustainable business model and shares results and experiences of companies who
have established programs.

14. "About Sunfunder," accessed January 2016, http://sunfunder
.com/company/.

15. Tom Randall, "Wind and Solar Are Crushing Fossil Fuels: Record Clean Energy Investment Outpaces Gas and Coal 2 to 1," *Bloomberg*,
April 6, 2016, https://www.bloomberg.com/news/articles/2016-04-06
/wind-and-solar-are-crushing-fossil-fuels.

16. "The Equator Principles," Equator Principles Association, 2011,
www.equator-principles.com.

17. "Sustainability at IFC, Risk Management: Performance Standards,"
The International Finance Corporation, accessed January 2017, www.ifc
.org/wps/wcm/connect/topics_ext_content/ifc_external_corporate_site
/ifc+sustainability/our+approach/risk+management/performance
+standards/environmental+and+social+performance+standards+and
+guidance+notes.

18. Climate Bonds Initiative, "Bonds and Climate Change: The State
of the Market in 2012," prepared for HSBC, June 2012, https://www
.climatebonds.net/files/uploads/2012/05/CB-HSBC_Final_30May12-A3
.pdf.

19. Climate Bonds Initiative, "Explaining Green Bonds," accessed
June 8, 2015, www.climatebonds.net/market/explaining-green-bonds.

20. Climate Bonds Initiative, "Bonds and Climate Change: The
State of the Market in 2014," prepared for HSBC, July 2014, https://www
.climatebonds.net/files/files/-CB-HSBC-15July2014-A5-final.pdf.

21. Climate Bonds Initiative, "Explaining Green Bonds."

22. Climate Bonds Initiative, "The State of the Market in 2014."

23. Mathew Thomas, "Asia Awakes to Green Bonds," *Emerging Mar-*

kets, February 5, 2015, http://www.emergingmarkets.org/Article/3450147
/Asia-awakes-to-green-bonds.html (site discontinued).

24. Ibid.

25. " Climate Bonds Initiative, "The State of the Market in 2014."

26. Ibid.

27. Global Sustainability Investment Alliance, "2014 Global Sustainability Investment Review," February 2015, http://www.gsi-alliance.org
/wp-content/uploads/2015/02/GSIA_Review_download.pdf.

28. Institutional Investors Group on Climate Change, "2009 Investor Statement on the Urgent Need for a Global Agreement on Climate Change," September 16, 2009, http://www.unepfi.org/fileadmin
/documents/need_agreement.pdf.

29. Institutional Investors Group on Climate Change, "2014/2015 Investor Statement on the Urgent Need for a Global Agreement on Climate Change," September 18, 2014, www.iigcc.org/publications/publication
/2014-global-investor-statement-on-climate-change.

30. Sean Kidney, "Insurers Worth $3.5tn Call for Climate Bonds and Support Standards," Climate Bonds Initiative, accessed December 6, 2011, www.climatebonds.net/2014/05/insurers-worth-35tn-call-climate
-bonds-and-support-standards.

31. Climate Bonds Initiative, "The State of the Market in 2014."

32. Sean Kidney and Padraig Oliver, "Growing a Green Bonds Market in China: Reducing Costs and Increasing Capacity for Green Investment While Promoting Greater Transparency and Stability in Financial Markets," International Institute for Sustainable Development, 2014, http://www
.iisd.org/sites/default/files/publications/growing_green_bonds_en.pdf.

33. "Can China Clean Up Fast Enough?," *The Economist*, August 10, 2013, http://www.economist.com/news/leaders/21583277-worlds-biggest
-polluter-going-green-it-needs-speed-up-transition-can-china.

34. OECD, "Green Growth and Developing Countries: A Summary for Policy Makers," June 2012, http://www.oecd.org/dac/50526354.pdf.

35. Stephen Minas, "Growth of Green Bonds Poses Challenges for Investors, Regulators," *Eco-Business*, December 1, 2014, www.eco
-business.com/opinion/growth-green-bonds-poses-challenges-investors
-regulators.

36. US White House, " Obama Administration Announces More Than $4 Billion in Private Sector Commitments and Executive Actions to Scale Up Investment in Clean Energy Innovation," press release, June 16, 2015,

https://obamawhitehouse.archives.gov/the-press-office/2015/06/16/fact
-sheet-obama-administration-announces-more-4-billion-private-sector.

37. Mark Boroush, "U.S. R&D Increased by More Than $20 Billion in Both 2013 and 2014, with Similar Increase Estimated for 2015," National Science Foundation, September 15, 2016, www.nsf.gov/statistics/2016 /nsf16316/.

38. "Historical Trends in Federal R&D," American Association for the Advancement of Science, accessed December 2017, www.aaas.org/page /historical-trends-federal-rd.

39. Jeffrey Mervis, "U.S. Research Groups Going to War Again over Small Business Funding," *Science Magazine*, May 18, 2016, www.sciencemag .org/news/2016/05/us-research-groups-going-war-again-over-small -business-funding.

40. Rachel Weiner, "Solyndra Explained," *Washington Post*, June 1, 2012, www.washingtonpost.com/blogs/the-fix/post/solyndra—explained /2012/06/01/gJQAig2g6U_blog.html.

41. "The Solyndra Failure," Majority Staff Report, US House of Representatives, 112th Congress, August 2, 2012, https://archives-energy commerce.house.gov/sites/republicans.energycommerce.house.gov /files/analysis/20120802solyndra.pdf.

42. Interestingly, in 2014, Wanxiang, a Chinese auto parts company backed by Chinese entrepreneur and billionaire Lu Guanqiu, purchased Fisker's assets out of bankruptcy for $149 million. Wanxiang relaunched Fisker as Karma Automotive, announcing its first offering in 2016, the Revero hybrid for $130,000.

43. "State Net Metering Policies," National Conference of State Legislatures, November 3, 2016, http://www.ncsl.org/research/energy/net -metering-policy-overview-and-state-legislative-updates.aspx.

44. Alexander E. MacDonald, Christopher T. M. Clack, Anneliese Alexander, Adam Dunbar, James Wilczak, and Yuanfu Xie, "Future Cost-Competitive Electricity Systems and Their Impact on US CO-2- Emissions," *Nature Climate Change* 6 (2016): 526–531, http://www.nature.com /nclimate/journal/v6/n5/full/nclimate2921.html.

45. Zia Wadud, Don MacKenzie, and Paul Leiby, "Help or Hindrance? The Travel, Energy and Carbon Impacts of Highly Automated Vehicles," Transportation Research Part A: Policy and Practice, *Science Direct* 86 (April 2016): 1–18, http://www.sciencedirect.com/science/article /pii/S0965856415002694.

46. "2013 Infrastructure Report Card," American Society of Civil Engineers, accessed October 2016, http://2013.infrastructurereportcard.org/.

47. "Examples of Successful Public-Private Partnerships," United Nations Office for South-South Cooperation, Global South-South Development Academy, Sharing Innovative Experiences, Vol. 15, chap. 8, http://academy.ssc.undp.org/GSSDAcademy/SIE/VOL15.aspx.

48. South African Wind Energy Association (SAWEA), "Reaping Reward—South Africa's REIPPP," November 4, 2015, http://www.energy.org.za/news/246-reaping-rewards-sa-reippp.

49. "Biomakers Consortium," Foundation for the National Institutes of Health, accessed November 2016, http://www.fnih.org/what-we-do/biomarkers-consortium.

50. Ian Hathaway, "Accelerating Growth: Startup Accelerator Programs in the United States," Brookings, February 17, 2016, www.brookings.edu/research/accelerating-growth-startup-accelerator-programs-in-the-united-states.

51. Carey Brauer, "The Business of Growing Business," *Panama City News Herald*, November 29, 2016, http://www.newsherald.com/news/20161119/business-of-growing-business.

52. Mike Hower, "Business Incubators Helping Sustainability Startups Thrive," Sustainable Brands, November 16, 2015, www.sustainablebrands.com/news_and_views/startups/mike_hower/business_incubators_help_sustainability_startups_thrive.

53. "National Clean Energy Incubators Spawn New Commercialization Centers," US Department of Energy, June 27, 2016, www.energy.gov/eere/ampedup/articles/national-clean-energy-incubators-spawn-new-commercialization-centers.

54. Chance Barnett, "Trends Show Crowdfunding to Surpass VC in 2016," *Forbes*, June 9, 2015, http://www.forbes.com/sites/chancebarnett/2015/06/09/trends-show-crowdfunding-to-surpass-vc-in-2016/2/#7948dfaf76da.

55. Amy Feldman, "Elio Motors, First Equity-Crowdfunded IPO, Soars Past $1B Valuation Days after Listing Shares," *Forbes*, March 1, 2016, www.forbes.com/sites/amyfeldman/2016/03/01/elio-motors-first-equity-crowdfunded-company-soars-past-1b-valuation-days-after-listing-shares/#6101922541cf.

56. Elio Motors, accessed November 2016, www.eliomotors.com. Eq-

uity crowdfunding enables people to invest in early start-up companies not yet listed on the public market and in return own a small share of the company.

57. David Bank, "CREO Investors Pledge $300 Million for Environmental Impact," *Huffington Post*, September 10, 2014, www.huffingtonpost.com/david-bank/creo-investors-pledge-300_b_5797346.html.

58. Margaret Collins, "Wealthy Families Unite at White House for Clean-Tech Push," *Private Wealth*, June 16, 2015, https://www.fa-mag.com/news/wealthy-families-unite-at-white-house-for-clean-tech-push-22141.html.

Chapter 5

1. "Smart Thermostat Market Analysis by Technology (Wi-Fi, Zig-Bee) and Segment Forecasts to 2022: Report Summary," Grand View Research, October 2016, www.grandviewresearch.com/industry-analysis/smart-thermostat-market.

2. Michael J. Coren, "2016 Was the Year Solar Panels Finally Became Cheaper Than Fossil Fuels. Just Wait for 2017," *Quartz*, December 26, 2016, https://qz.com/871907/2016-was-the-year-solar-panels-finally-became-cheaper-than-fossil-fuels-just-wait-for-2017/.

3. "Consumer-Goods' Brands That Demonstrate Commitment to Sustainability Outperform Those That Don't," press release, Nielsen Company, October 12, 2015, http://www.nielsen.com/us/en/press-room/2015/consumer-goods-brands-that-demonstrate-commitment-to-sustainability-outperform.html.

4. Renée Shaw Hughner, Pierre McDonagh, Andrea Prothero, Clifford J. Shultz II, and Julie Stanton, "Who Are Organic Food Consumers? A Compilation and Review of Why People Purchase Organic Food," *Journal of Consumer Behavior* 6 (2007): 94–110, doi:10.1002/cb.210.

5. Geertje Schuitema and Judith I. M. de Groot, "Green Consumerism: The Influence of Product Attributes and Values on Purchasing Intentions, Journal of Consumer Behavior 14, no. 1 (2015): 57–69, doi:10.1002/cb.1501.

6. Jack Neff, "As More Marketers Go Green, Fewer Consumers Willing to Pay for It," *AdvertisingAge*, September 24, 2012, http://adage.com/article/news/marketers-green-fewer-consumers-pay/237377/.

7. Marcello Graziano and Kenneth Gillingham, "Spatial Patterns of Solar Photovoltaic System Adoption: The Influence of Neighbors and the Built Environment," *Journal of Economic Geography* 15, no. 4 (2014): 815–839.

8. Dora L. Costa and Matthew E. Kahn, "Energy Conservation 'Nudges' and Environmentalist Ideology: Evidence from a Randomized Residential Electricity Field Experiment," *Journal of the European Economic Association* 11, no. 3 (2013): 680–702.

9. Suzanne Snowdon and Poh-Khim Cheah, *Redefining Business Success in a Changing World: CEO Survey*, PwC Global, January 2016, 12–17, https://www.pwc.com/gx/en/ceo-survey/2016/landing-page/pwc-19th-annual-global-ceo-survey.pdf.

10. "Green Household Cleaning and Laundry Products in the U.S., 3rd Edition," Packaged Facts, March 13, 2015, www.packagedfacts.com/Green-Household-Cleaning-8825323.

11. Steve French, "Market Insights from Top Researchers: The Latest Intelligence on Customer Attitudes and Behavior," Natural Marketing Institute, November 19, 2015, www.sustainablebrands.com/digital_learning/slideshow/behavior_change/market_insights_top_researchers_latest_intelligence_custo.

12. "Overview of Awards by FY 2008–2016," USA Spending. gov, 2016, www.usaspending.gov/transparency/Pages/OverviewOfAwards.aspx.

13. US Department of Energy, "ENERGY STAR and FEMP-Designated Products Procurement Requirements," accessed October 2016, https://www4.eere.energy.gov/femp/requirements/laws_and_requirements/energy_star_and_femp_designated_products_procurement_requirements.

14. "General Government Final Consumption Expenditure (% of GDP) [United States]," World Bank, accessed November 2016, data.worldbank.org/indicator/NE.CON.GOVT.ZS?locations=US.

15. "Solar Investment Tax Credit (ITC)," Solar Energy Industries Association, accessed September 5, 2017, www.seia.org/policy/finance-tax/solar-investment-tax-credit.

16. Emily Cassidy, "Ethanol's Broken Promise: Using Less Corn Ethanol Reduces Greenhouse Gas Emissions," Environmental Working Group, May 2014, http://www.ewg.org/research/ethanols-broken-promise.

17. Scott Drenkard, "How High Are Cigarette Taxes in Your State?," *Tax Foundation* (blog), March 28, 2016, taxfoundation.org/blog/how-high-are-cigarette-taxes-your-state-0.

18. "Cigarette Smoking Adults, 1965–2012," Office of Disease Prevention and Health Promotion, revised August 25, 2014, www.healthypeople.gov/2020/topics-objectives/national-snapshot/cigarette-smoking-adults-1965%E2%80%932012.

19. Centers for Disease Control and Prevention, "Youth Risk Behav-

ior Surveillance—United States, 2015," *Surveillance Summaries* 65, no. 6 (2016): 14, www.cdc.gov/healthyyouth.

20. Urban Institute and Brookings Institution, Tax Policy Center Statistics, "State Motor Fuels Tax Rates 2000–2011, 2013–2017," February 9, 2017, http://www.taxpolicycenter.org/statistics/state-motor-fuels-tax-rates -2000-2011-2013-2017.

21. "Short-Term Energy Outlook: Real Prices Viewer, 2006 and 2016 Nominal Prices," US Energy Information Administration, accessed October 2017, www.eia.gov/forecasts/steo/realprices/.

22. Jurgen Weiss, "Solar Energy Support in Germany: A Closer Look," Solar Energy Industries Association, July 2014, http://www.seia.org /research-resources/solar-energy-support-germany-closer-look.

23. DSIRE database, operated by the NC Clean Energy Technology Center and funded by the US DOE, "Renewable Portfolio Standard Policies," data from March 2015, http://ncsolarcen-prod.s3.amazonaws.com /wp-content/uploads/2017/03/Renewable-Portfolio-Standards.pdf.

24. Office of Transportation and Air Quality U.S. Environmental Protection Agency, National Highway Traffic Safety Administration U.S. Department of Transportation and California Air Resources Board, "Draft Technical Assessment Report: Midterm Evaluation of Light-Duty Vehicle Greenhouse Gas Emission Standards and Corporate Average Fuel Economy Standards for Model Years 2022–2025," July 2016, https:// www.nhtsa.gov/corporate-average-fuel-economy/light-duty-cafe-midterm -evaluation. At the time of publication, EPA and NHTSA had conducted a technical assessment to evaluate fuel economy improvements and the auto industry's ability to meet future standards using existing and new technologies. EPA is scheduled to issue a Final Determination by April 2018, followed by a joint Final Rule prior to 2022. http://www.nhtsa.gov /Laws+&+Regulations/CAFE+-+Fuel+Economy/ld-cafe-midterm -evaluation-2022-25

25. National Highway Traffic Safety Administration, "Obama Administration Finalizes Historic 54.5 mpg Fuel Efficiency Standards," news release, August 28, 2012, https://one.nhtsa.gov/About-NHTSA/Press -Releases/2012/Obama-Administration-Finalizes-Historic-54.5-mpg -Fuel-Efficiency-Standards.

26. "Table 4-23: Average Fuel Efficiency of U.S. Light Duty Vehicles," US Department of Transportation, Bureau of Transportation Statistics, accessed September 2016, www.rita.dot.gov/bts/sites/rita.dot.gov.bts

/files/publications/national_transportation_statistics/html/table_04
_23.html.

27. Office of Transportation and Air Quality U.S. Environmental Protection Agency, National Highway Traffic Safety Administration U.S. Department of Transportation and California Air Resources Board, "Draft Technical Assessment Report."

28. "Organic Market Overview," US Department of Agriculture Economic Research Service, Natural Resources and Environment: Organic Agriculture, April 4, 2017, https://www.ers.usda.gov/topics/natural -resources-environment/organic-agriculture/organic-market-overview .aspx.

29. "U.S. Organic Trade Industry 2016," Organic Trade Association, accessed September 5, 2017, www.ota.com/resources/market-analysis.

30. Marine Stewardship Council, accessed December 2016, www.msc .org.

31. Forest Stewardship Council, accessed December 2016, www.us.fsc .org.

32. James Maxwell and Forrest Brisco, "There's Money in the Air: The CFC Ban and DuPont's Regulatory Strategy," *Business Strategy and the Environment* 6 (1997): 276–286.

33. "Annual Lobbying by Exxon Mobil [2015]," Center for Responsive Politics, accessed October 2016, http://www.opensecrets.org/lobby /clientsum.php?id=D000000129&year=2015.

34. "Annual Lobbying on Oil & Gas [2015]," Center for Responsive Politics, accessed October 2016, http://www.opensecrets.org/lobby /indusclient.php?id=E01&year=2015.

35. Ibid.

36. Michael Lenox and Chuck Eesley, "Private Environmental Activism and the Selection and Response of Firm Targets," *Journal of Economics & Management Strategy* 18, no. 1 (2009): 45–73.

37. Eric Hoffmann, "Coming to a Grocery Store near You: Campaign for GE-Free Seafood," *Friends of the Earth* (blog), March 20, 2013, https:// foe.org/2013-03-campaign-for-gefree-seafood/.

38. Robert Mclean and Irene Chapple, "BP Settles Final Gulf Oil Spill Claims for $20 Billion," *CNN Money*, October 6, 2015, money.cnn .com/2015/10/06/news/companies/deepwater-horizon-bp-settlement/.

39. Kim Bhasin, "BP Is Spending $500 Million to Fix Its Brand and Get Everybody to Forget about Deepwater Horizon," *Business Insider*, Febru-

ary 3, 2012, www.businessinsider.com/bp-is-spending-500-million-to-fix
-its-brand-and-get-everybody-to-forget-about-deepwater-horizon-2012-2.

40. Rick Wagoner, guest lecture in course "Managing Radical Technology Change," Duke University, September 2004.

41. "What Is BPA, and What Are the Concerns about BPA?," Mayo Clinic, accessed January 2017, http://www.mayoclinic.org/healthy-lifestyle/nutrition-and-healthy-eating/expert-answers/bpa/faq-20058331.

Chapter 6

1. Danielle Wiener-Bronner, "Tesla Just Became the Most Valuable Carmaker in America," *CNN Money*, April 11, 2017, http://money.cnn.com/2017/04/10/investing/tesla-gm-market-cap/index.html.

2. Vanessa Kirsch, Jim Bildner, and Jeff Walker, "Why Social Ventures Need Systems Thinking," *Harvard Business Review*, July 25, 2016, https://hbr.org/2016/07/why-social-ventures-need-systems-thinking.

3. Eric Holthaus, "Hot Zone: Is Climate Change Destabilizing Iraq?," *Slate*, June 27, 2014, http://www.slate.com/articles/technology/future_tense/2014/06/isis_water_scarcity_is_climate_change_destabilizing_iraq.html.

INDEX

Page numbers in italic indicate material in figures.